Rescuer
by Night

Rescuer
by Night

Amy Carmichael

Kay Walsh

CF4•K

Copyright © 2004 Kay Walsh
Reprinted 2008 and 2012
ISBN 978-1-85792-946-1

Published by
Christian Focus Publications,
Geanies House, Fearn, Tain, Ross-shire,
IV20 1TW, Scotland, U.K.

www.christianfocus.com
email: info@christianfocus.com
Thinking further topics; timeline and life summary
Copyright © Christian Focus Publications

Cover design by Alister MacInnes
Cover illustration by Helen Smith

Printed and bound in Denmark
by Nørhaven

For Ilona,
whose service in India
helped in the writing of
Amy's story

Contents

Into the Dark

'I can't see! It's dark everywhere. What place is this? Where am I?' Jeya tried to peer about her. Her mouth felt dry. She knew she must have been asleep for a long time as she now felt very hungry and thirsty. As her eyes got used to the dark she could make out large stone pillars. Strange, unearthly shapes reared up out of the gloom. Between the pillars was a huge stone body. She shivered when she saw its face. The stern, angry features were decorated with red and black markings. This, she knew, was Kali, the goddess of death and destruction.

The little girl trembled. She realised that she must be in a temple. She tried to move, but her legs were tied together. The bars of her cage were thick and strong. She tried to remember what she had heard the priest say to her mother.

'Your little girl will be happy with us. She will have plenty of food. We will teach her to dance before our gods. She will gain heaven for all your family by pleasing the gods.'

'I'm not sure about this now. When I agreed the other day I wasn't thinking. My Jeya is so young and tiny.' Her mother sounded worried and afraid. The priest's narrow eyes flickered with anger as she said this.

'But I have brought the money with me. Your other children will have a better home and good food. How can a poor widow like you give three children all that? Now don't argue any more. We have an agreement!'

Jeya could see the tears in her mother's eyes. She heard again the clinking sound as money was handed over. A last hug from her mother and she was gone. The priest lifted the four-year-old he had bought onto his cart and they left her home. On the journey he gave her something to drink, sweet and sticky. After that she felt very drowsy and must have fallen asleep.

'Wake up, girl! I've come to fetch you.' Piercing eyes were staring in at Jeya. A small, thin woman had stepped forward in front of the cage. She was very old and her dark-brown skin was wrinkled and leathery.

She lifted a latch outside and put her hands in to untie the cloth bands around Jeya's legs. 'Come with me,' she ordered. 'You will spend your first few months with me at my home and find out your temple duties.'

Her hut was dirty and smelly. She gave the little girl two meals a day and began making her learn by heart the long chants to say to the gods. If Jeya made a mistake the old woman slapped her hard. 'How is my mother? Is my little brother well again?' she asked the woman. 'Forget all about them. Your life is here now. You must work hard or the priest will beat you.' Jeya sobbed herself to sleep every night.

Every afternoon the woman sent her to fetch water from the river while she had a good long nap. On her sixth day there Jeya was down at the river on her own. She sat on the riverbank a little longer than usual. The water-pot was heavy and she had already made three long trips with it.

'You look tired, little one. Someone who loves you has told me that you have been sold to the priest. I can take you away from here to a safe place.' The voice was soft and friendly. Jeya looked up into a smiling face. The woman's dark-brown eyes gazing down at her made her look so kind. 'We can travel in the bullock-cart over there,' she said.

Jeya looked to where she pointed and saw an older woman and a driver waiting near the trees. No more chanting, or beatings, or working in that frightening temple. 'Oh, yes please,' she replied. The woman in the sari picked her up and carried her over to the cart.

After travelling for several hours they arrived at a low building behind a bungalow. Jeya was so tired she hardly took in her new surroundings. The older woman now spoke. 'Amy, you put her to bed and I will fetch a cup of milk for her.' Jeya was carried to a bedroom, undressed and placed in a cot by the same woman who had spoken to her by the river.

Suddenly, all Jeya's fears returned and she cried out, 'You won't beat me, will you? I'll be good and work hard for you!' To her surprise she felt the woman's arms around her and a gentle voice said, 'You will not be made to work hard here. Tonight you will sleep in my room. You will have brothers and sisters to play with in the garden tomorrow. Our God is love. No one will hurt you here.'

Although the woman's eyes were brown, Jeya could now see that she did not have brown skin. 'Why have you come here? What is your name? Are you from a village over the mountains?' Jeya asked her. At this the woman laughed and said, 'My name is Amy Carmichael, but you can call me Amma. My home is over the mountains and over the sea, too. Big ships sailed across stormy waters to bring me to this place. I come from a country called Great Britain. Now you close your eyes and I will introduce you to your new friends in the morning.'

Jeya felt less afraid now. Her bed was soft and the milk had been so good. She began to feel sleepy. 'Over the sea, that sounds a long way away,' she thought, 'I wonder what the sea is? Is it safe? Perhaps it is dangerous? But I don't have to worry about things like that. I know that this lady is going to look after me. I've never felt so safe before – I'm going to like it here.' And the little girl closed her eyes and drifted off to sleep.

Saved

'Help! Help! We're caught in the tide. The current's too strong for us,' Norman yelled. He gripped his oar even tighter. So did his brother, Ernest. Their sister Amy just froze on the spot and wondered what their parents were going to say when they found out that they'd been disobedient. How many times had the Carmichael children been told, "The ocean is dangerous. Be careful and don't on any account take the boat out on your own!" But Amy, Norman and Ernest just hadn't listened and now they wished that they had. The dark green waters of the lake had them in its clutches and the children were being blown rapidly away from the safety of the harbour.

Both boys knew they were being drawn nearer to the sandbar at the entrance. Beyond that lay the open waters of the Irish Sea.

'Hold on as tightly as you can, Amy,' the boys called to their sister. She did as they said. 'I will, I will. We've rowed here before and it was fine. We must have somehow come a bit further down. It's nearly evening-time. Perhaps the tide is different then,' Amy replied.

Norman was thinking hard. 'Amy, you start singing at the top of your voice. Someone may hear us. Ernest and I must keep rowing. We may be able to slow the boat down enough to stop ourselves reaching the sea.' Amy began singing,

"Whatever I do, whatever I be,

Still I know it's God's hand that's leading me."

The hymn was the first thing that came into her head. By now dark clouds had formed above them. How small their boat seemed on the rough waters of the lake.

'I can see something at the edge. I think it's a boat. Yes, it's the coastguards! Over here. We're over here. They're coming. We're saved!' shouted Amy.

How happy the three felt to reach home safely that night. An exhausted Amy wriggled down to get comfortable in her bed. She loved their old house with its grey stone walls. Listening to the roar of the wind outside made the bedroom really cosy.

It wasn't long, though, before the children were in trouble again. Their father was part-owner of the large flour-mill in their seaside village. This meant he could afford a large house and garden. There Amy and her four brothers and two sisters could play as much as they liked. She loved all the flowers and trees but could not help experimenting with some of them. One day they were enjoying some ripe plums from the garden. 'Let's eat the stones as well,' suggested Amy.

'Stop that! I can see what you're doing.' The children looked up. Their nursemaid, Bessie, was standing by the back door. 'If you swallow those, a plum tree will grow out of your head, for every one you've eaten.'

'I don't like the sound of that,' said one.

'I'm going to eat twelve stones and see if I have twelve trees growing out of my head tomorrow,' declared Amy defiantly. Next morning a worried Bessie asked, 'Are you all right, Amy?'

'No I've got a stomach pain that feels as if twelve plum trees are growing inside me.'

Not that this taught her a lesson. A few days later Norman, Ernest and Amy were swinging on the front gate. Above them the bright yellow tassels of the laburnum tree blew to and fro. "Bessie says silly things just to scare us, I'm sure. She told us if we ate laburnum pods we would die. Let's count how many we can eat before we die,' said Amy. As usual, the other two joined in with her.

A few minutes later all three began to feel queasy. Ernest, the youngest, had turned very pale. He ran indoors. 'Mother, I feel ill and sort of peculiar. I think it's eating the laburnum that's done it.'

Mrs Carmichael ran towards him in alarm. 'Amy, Norman, come into the dining-room quickly!' There, on a tray, was the pink powder they all knew and dreaded. She filled three tea-cups with hot water and stirred in the powder. They all knew just how foul this would taste.

'Drink it all down, to the last drop. We'll soon have that poison out of your system.' Their mother was right about that! All three were very, very, sick and felt very, very, glad that their punishment was to be sent to bed early, without having to eat their supper.

Next morning Amy stepped outside and took a deep breath. 'I feel much better now,' she thought, 'Mother did give me a good old telling-off, though. I suppose I deserved it, I am the eldest. Still, if only she knew how much naughtier I could be, she wouldn't think I'm naughty at all.'

Just then she heard 'plop' in the bucket by the door. She looked in and there was a little field-mouse. 'Oh, I can't let you drown. Oh, no! There's the bell for prayers. I must be on time or there'll be more trouble.' Saying this, she quickly scooped up the mouse from the water and hid him in her apron pocket.

She took her place at the table and her father began praying. After the Lord's prayer which they all said together, he read a Bible story to them. Just as he began praying for the family and their friends, a squeaking noise started up. Everyone turned to look at Amy.

'It was going to drown. I just thought it would be quiet.'

Her younger brothers and sisters began to giggle. She turned and ran out to the garden where she set the mouse free.

'It's no wonder the governesses I employ to teach you don't stay very long,' her father told his family when all the commotion had died down. 'That poor English woman stayed the shortest time of all. I remember you all went to see her off. Why did you do that? I know you didn't like her.'

'We just wanted to be sure she went,' explained Amy.

Amy's father laughed, 'What mischievous children you are!'

One morning Amy's father had some interesting news. 'We are going to have a new neighbour,' her father told them. 'He is a missionary in India but he and his family are taking a year's leave. I'm sure he will have lots of fascinating stories to tell you so behave yourselves when he is here.'

Fortunately for her parents, one of Amy's worst escapades happened before the new people moved in. She knew her brothers, like her, had a very special place they wanted to climb – the roof. They decided to clamber up through the bathroom skylight. This skylight was right above the bath and it was quite narrow. Amy had to give each brother a hard push through the window before squeezing through herself. One by one they slid down the slate roof onto the lead gutter.

'What a view!" exclaimed Amy as she gazed out to sea. Deep fathomless blue water glinted in the sunshine. The Irish Sea was quite a sight - especially from the top of a roof.

All three then marched round the roof - laughing and giggling. This game was great fun, they thought. When they reached the front of the house they looked down again. What view would they get from this angle they wondered. It was a view that none of them had expected. Amy gasped. So did her parents!

'Stay where you are,' their father yelled. 'I'm coming up to the bathroom to get you.' Minutes later Amy and her brothers were clambering through the skylight again and listening to yet another telling off.

Headstrong, daring, wild – Amy had heard all these descriptions of herself. Now, as she sat on the large chair in her mother's room, she thought over some of her past exploits. 'I have been very wilful, but I don't really feel sorry at all, I enjoy doing exciting things.'

But Amy didn't realise that although these things were exciting for her – one person in the house was very worried. Her mother was sitting at the dressing-table mirror, putting on a hat.

'What are you doing?' Amy asked her.

'I am getting ready to go out,' was her mother's quiet reply.

Amy glanced at her mother's reflection and saw the tired, hurt look on her face, 'Did I put that look there?' Amy wondered and then when she looked once more at her mother's sombre eyes Amy caught her breath. 'What have I done?' Sobbing, Amy ran across the room and flung herself into her mother's arms.

'I am truly sorry. I can't bear to hurt you. I want to be good.'

Amy's mother leaned over to hug her young impetuous daughter.

"Hush now. It's alright. I know you mean well. I just wish you took more care. I have far too many grey hairs already!' Amy's mother laughed as she looked at the mirror once more.

Amy sniffed quietly and smiled through her tears.

'I will stop all these foolish adventures and silly scrapes,' she promised herself. But, of course, Amy did not drop all her old ways at once. She did however, begin to help her mother with the younger children and tried to save her pain by behaving better – most of the time. To get rid of some of her boundless supply of energy Amy went on lots of pony rides. She loved to gallop over the firm sands of the nearby beach, her thick brown hair bobbing behind her. If the pony was suddenly frightened, she could soothe him by singing quietly in his ear. But when she was out riding on the main road one day this little trick of Amy's didn't work. The pony reared and bucked and eventually threw his young rider straight into the side of a wall. Amy's body crashed against it and then lay there, badly injured, as the pony vanished on the horizon. Amy was barely aware of the hushed whispers of the worried doctors who came to treat her. 'She'll be in bed for several weeks,' was the diagnosis. 'It's a serious accident.' But, when the injuries were healed and the young girl had recovered, she was soon out riding again.

And it was one day when Amy was returning from another energetic pony ride that she overheard her parents' plans for her future.

'Amy will be twelve years old soon,' her father said, nodding. 'She is definitely old enough to go to boarding school and England isn't that far away. I believe it's just what our young girl needs.'

Amy felt intrigued. 'Boarding-school might be fun,' she thought to herself. However, when she finally arrived there in 1879 Amy found that she was in fact very homesick … very homesick indeed.

'I want to go home!' she sobbed into her dormitory pillow one night. 'I want the beach and the boat and my pony and the laburnum tree. I want to climb the roof and play with my brothers. I miss everyone so much!"

The whole week at boarding school was very difficult for Amy. There wasn't a single day when she didn't miss Ireland. But of all the days in the week Sunday was the hardest of them all.

In Ireland, every Sunday morning her grandmother had made up a bunch of sweet-smelling flowers for her.

'I remember being very little and holding these flowers in church. They were the only thing that could keep me sitting still during the long service.' Amy sighed once more. 'I don't think boarding school is fun at all,' she moaned. 'There are no boys here and everyone is really strict! I even miss helping mother serve the soup to the old people in the village. It's funny how it's the ordinary things that I miss the most. Like our Sunday walks with Father and stroking Daisy the cat. The only lesson that's any good here is biology. I suppose that's because I love flowers so much.'

Thankfully Amy's mother knew how much her daughter loved flowers and sent Amy a box of colourful chrysanthemums from her greenhouse to cheer her up. So as time went on, Amy became less lonely, settled in and, to her surprise, became popular with the other girls. In a way that was what really led Amy into her next prank and into getting into some trouble with the headmistress.

'I've heard this comet will be the sight of a lifetime. Everyone will be watching it,' Amy's friend Meg was saying to her. 'A pity it has to be passing over here after midnight. Perhaps the Head will let us stay up late to see it. You ask her, Amy. You've got more nerve than any of us.'

Five minutes later Amy was back from the Head's room. 'She turned the idea down flat. Still, I have an idea of my own. If I arrange to wake everyone in our dormitory in time to see it, why don't we go up to the attic? There's sure to be a good view through that large skylight.'

'That's great!' said Meg, 'Let's do it. But how are we going to stay awake?'

'Well, here's my plan,' Amy whispered. 'I've cut all these lengths of cotton and I'll tie one to each of your toes.'

'Our toes?' Meg exclaimed.

'Yes, listen and I'll tell you why. Once you are all asleep I will stay awake and when it's time to go up to the attic I'll pull all the threads, you'll feel a tug on your toe and you'll all wake up just in time for the show.'

'That's a brilliant idea Amy,' Meg declared. 'I can't wait to tell the others.'

Once all the girls were tucked up in bed with their cotton threads attached to their toes Amy settled down to wait for the all clear. As soon as she was certain that the teachers must have all gone to sleep she pulled the threads and woke the dorm up. Quickly and silently all the girls tip-toed up to the attic.

However, as the girls stepped into the room, they had two surprises. First, they saw the splendour of the comet against the clear night sky. Secondly, they saw their Headmistress and four teachers standing there, also looking at it. The headmistress gasped and then quickly put two and two together. 'Amy – in my study 9 am tomorrow. I daresay you're the ringleader. Am I right? Back to bed all of you this instant!'

Amy sighed and headed off to the dormitory with the others. 'It's not fair. I'm always getting into trouble,' she grumbled.

The following morning she left the head's office with a very shamefaced look on her face. 'The head was right. I am almost fifteen years old. I shouldn't be getting into scrapes at my age. Perhaps now is the time to ask God to help me grow up,' she thought. But just after her fifteenth birthday something even better happened.

At a meeting that Amy and some school friends went to, the congregation sang one of Amy's favourite hymns. It was her mother's favourite hymn too: 'Jesus loves me, this I know, for the Bible tells me so.'

Amy found herself thinking about the words, trying to work out what they really meant. 'I've always known Jesus loves me, but it was mother who made that real. I can't always rely on my mother's faith,' Amy told herself. 'I've never really thought about how I should love Jesus myself.'

Mr and Mrs Carmichael were thrilled to have a letter from Amy a few days later telling them how she knew for sure she had been forgiven by 'the mercy of the Good Shepherd' as she put it.

Amy felt that this little hymn was the best news that she had ever heard and it was … but later that year she received some more good news of a different sort. 'No more boarding school. Yippee!' she yelled as she ran around the dormitory waving her parent's latest letter. 'I'm going home to Ireland.'

But even though the news was good for Amy, it was bad news for the family. The reason that Amy and her brothers were coming home was that the family business was going badly. Soon they had to move to Belfast where her father set up a smaller business and the children went to local schools.

Then one morning Amy's mother came into her room with some startling news. 'Pneumonia?' Amy gasped.

Her mother nodded. Her face was pale, her lips clasped tightly. 'Father has pneumonia.'

'People recover from pneumonia sometimes,' Amy told her mother. But over the following days and weeks Amy's father grew worse rather than better and just when the family needed the most help, financial disaster loomed.

Amy ran into the garden to hide behind the plum tree. 'We're ruined,' she sobbed. 'That man owes father lots of money but he can't or won't pay. But Mother mustn't see me crying like this,' she scolded herself.

However, that evening Amy was sobbing once again into her pillow. The pneumonia hadn't been cured. Mr Carmichael had died.

After the funeral was over and the coffin buried beneath the dark brown Irish soil, Amy found her life far, far different to what it had once been. Before she had been one of the children. Now she was the one her little brothers and sisters turned to with their worries and anxieties.

Who listened to Amy's troubles? Who helped her when every day she wanted to run into someone's arms and never let go? Every day she found the words of the Bible helped her to cope. 'God is a father to the fatherless.'

She knew that for a fact. She was beginning to grow up. She was beginning to trust in God.

The Shawlies

But Amy still had some wild ideas. 'My first idea today is - let's open a shop of our own.'

Amy's family looked doubtful. 'Won't we need a counter and a till and lots of expensive things to sell?' asked Norman.

'No,' said Amy, 'The shop is just for us. We'll run it at home. We can buy pens, pencils or make things to sell to relatives. You young ones will learn how to cope with money.'

'And my second idea is to produce a family magazine! It can have funny stories, drawings, articles on outings and hobbies, cartoons and all sorts, whatever we like.'

'I think we'll need a lot of paper and pens for it,' said Ernest. 'Let's all pay six pence a year towards running it. But first we'll have a vote to see if everyone wants to open a shop and run a magazine.'

Everyone agreed and Amy soon had them all busy and happy again. She smiled to herself as her brothers got stuck into their writing and drawing. 'I thought we'd never be happy in Belfast, but I was wrong,' Amy decided. 'Belfast is just different, that's all. But it is different, very different.'

Amy remembered the little seaside village that they had left behind. Small cottages, narrow twisting streets and row upon row of fishing nets. These had all been replaced by Belfast's tenements, dark cobbled back streets and the mills and factories packed with poor and struggling workers.

'Poverty is everywhere,' sighed Amy. 'It's ugly and it's the one part of this city that I hate. But what can I do about it?' she wondered. Then one cold, wet, morning, on their way home from church, Amy, Norman and Ernest noticed an old woman. She was poorly-dressed for the damp weather and was struggling to carry a heavy bundle.

'Come on,' Amy urged the others. 'She needs help.'

The youngsters immediately ran across the road to give the woman a hand. The boys took hold of the bundle and then all three helped her along by the arms and took her home. Other bystanders stared disapprovingly at them. Amy blushed. She felt their displeasure as they glared at her.

'I suppose they don't approve of a young girl like me helping someone from a poorer class.' But Amy realised what a foolish thought that was. 'She's just like any other old lady. She needs our help and it's not her fault that she's poor.'

Just as they passed a large fountain in the street, Amy remembered a Bible verse that she had learned. Paul had written to the Christians in a wealthy Greek city, Corinth, about the work they could do to serve God. If they built their work on Jesus himself it would be like gold and last forever. Amy felt as if a voice had spoken directly to her. She went home and spent the whole afternoon alone in her room, thinking about what God wanted her to do.

'I must find out more about the Belfast people. So many are poor and I don't have a clue about how I can help! I've never thought about poverty before. I suppose it was seeing that old woman struggling on her own that changed all that.' Just then Amy had an idea - 'I'll go and visit Dr Montgomery.'

Dr Montgomery was puzzled when he heard that a young girl wished to see him. He was a mission worker in the city and didn't often get visits from middle-class girls like Amy Carmichael. 'Show her in,' he told his secretary. 'I wonder what she wants?'

Amy came straight to the point. 'I need to know more about the way people live in the back streets. I want to do something to help them and show them the love of Jesus.'

Dr Montgomery wasn't certain about this. He had to find out if Amy realised how awful this work might be. 'Do you know what you'd be letting yourself in for?' he asked.

'I think I do,' Amy replied. 'I have been there and have talked to the girls,' she told him, 'Some come home with me for a Bible meeting on Sunday. Mother and I give them something to eat before they leave. But they don't even know how to read and write. How do I help these girls?'

Dr Montgomery smiled. 'I have an idea of how you can help some boys. My daughter is like you. Perhaps you two would like to teach a group of young boys. They have to work all day but we could set up a night school for them.'

'That's a brilliant idea,' Amy exclaimed. For the next year she was very busy … very busy indeed.

'There's just so much to do,' sighed Amy some months later. There had been a Bible class on the Sunday and a night school on the Monday and now Amy was walking down one of the Belfast back streets - she'd had yet another idea.

'Look at these girls,' she muttered to herself. 'They look chilled to the bone and tired out. The weather is freezing and none of them has a hat. All they have to keep the rain off them are thread-bare shawls. That's how they get their nickname, 'Shawlies'. We must do something to help them.'

Amy ran across the road to speak to one girl huddled in a doorway. 'It makes me mad how so called respectable people have nothing to do with these girls!'

And that night, after Amy waved goodbye to the Belfast Shawlies, she stopped off at the minister's house for a chat.

'I want to help the shawlies,' she began. 'Could we have a special meeting just for them? As they work such long hours I'll have to get them together on Sunday mornings. Could I use our church hall to do this?'

'Has your mother agreed?' he asked.

'Oh, yes,' Amy replied, 'she thinks it's an excellent idea.'

'Your mother is a remarkable woman. My own wife has said she wouldn't let one of our children go down the streets you enter. But I will help you. You can use the hall.'

Amy was delighted and threw herself into providing a cheerful, enjoyable time for the shawlies. They loved her and soon encouraged their friends to join them. As she wanted to give them a real chance in life, she included sewing and singing in week-day meetings, too. However, teaching them about the Saviour she loved was most important to her. After a while friends saw she needed a rest.

'Amy is tiring herself out,' someone said. 'Let's send her on a holiday.'

'What a good idea. But where to?'

'How about Scotland? It's not too far away.'

So Scotland it was.

But at a meeting in Glasgow she felt challenged over what she gave to the work in Belfast. 'The preacher asked if our work was lasting like gold or if it was going to vanish at the first puff of wind. Am I relying on my own efforts too much? I work so hard, I have all these ideas … but I haven't been trusting in God as I should have been. It is God who is the strong one. Not me.'

Amy realised that she had to trust in God completely. If it was his work he would help her. So instead of sending Amy away on holiday her friends had sent her to somewhere that made her want to do God's work even more. However, on her return from Scotland Amy's mother had some difficult news for her. '… As you know, when father died we did not have a lot of money and now most of that has gone too. We need to pray for help. God will provide but we must be careful with what we spend.'

So between them the Carmichaels counted the pennies and began to save even more than they had been already.

Amy had other problems, too. Sadly, some church members were opposed to so many shawlies using their hall. It was clear that the hall was no longer big enough for all the shawlies. The solution was obvious to Amy.

'I have to build a new hall.'

'How can you possibly do that?' Ernest responded. 'You'll need to buy land and have a building put up.'

'It is God's work. It can be done, I'm sure. Did you know that you can build an iron hall for £500? I know that God answers prayers. Just look at my Ask and Receive book.'

Ernest smiled as he looked at his sister's well-worn notebook. Every item she asked for and every item she received was carefully inserted into the columns of the book. Amy's neat handwriting listed out all her prayer requests and answers. Of course, Amy knew that not all answers to prayer were yes and she tried to remember that too. However, Amy had quite an encouraging reaction to her plans when visiting a friend of her mother.

'You know, I think I may be able to help you. I have a friend, a Miss Mitchell, who lost a sister recently. She is wealthy and has decided to do something in her memory.'

To Amy's surprise Miss Mitchell invited her to lunch. A butler opened the door and Amy was shown into a sunny room looking on to a garden. Never shy, Amy was soon telling Miss Mitchell all about 'her' shawlies. Three days later a note arrived, offering to pay for the hall.

'You still need land to build on,' someone said. 'Ask a mill owner for some. After all, the girls work for them.'

So Amy did just that. An owner agreed to rent some land to her for a small amount and by January 1889, the hall was ready. Amy called it 'The Welcome' and sent out invitations to the opening with a little verse on the front:

> 'Come one, Come all,
> To the Welcome Hall.
> And come in your working clothes.'

The new hall held five hundred. After the opening, a puzzled friend asked her, 'I didn't see you on the platform. Where were you?'

'Oh no,' she replied, 'I was in the audience.' It was just like Amy to be alongside the women and not above them. She was a friend and not just a woman who told them stories.

But it wasn't only shawlies that Amy would make friends with that year. When Amy's mother was offered a job as a superintendent of a women's refuge it meant that Amy had to leave Belfast to go with her mother to Manchester in England. Amy had to make new friends and begin a new work. At first she worried if it was the right course of action. As she packed up much loved books, photographs and other personal belongings she felt anxious. But then a sense of calm came. 'This is the right decision,' she declared. 'It makes sense. After all, the boys are going abroad to work and there is work in Manchester for both mother and me. I can work with factory girls this time. Mother is going to let me rent a room downtown. It will be closer to my work… even though it is a bit of a rough area.' And rough it was…

At night the street was filled with shouts and screams as drunken fights broke out. At break of day the factory sirens blared and the workers clattered down the cobbled streets in their wooden clogs. Black smoke from factory chimneys caused a stench on the streets and this made breathing difficult. Amy's room was dirty and smelly and fleas and cockroaches lived in the walls. But Amy knew sharing this way of life with the girls was just another way to help them.

However, one evening, as she walked home by herself, a group of rowdy young men began to follow her. They jeered and swore at her. Never one to give in to fear, Amy continued walking at the same pace. Things turned really nasty, though, as it became clear they intended harming her. Suddenly, a woman standing in a doorway dashed into the mob and pulled Amy by the hand into her house.

'Get away you dirty scoundrels,' Amy's rescuer yelled. 'Just wait till my man gets home.' Her 'man' must have been quite a frightening prospect as her threatening words sent them skulking away, muttering to each other.

As Amy crept in the door to her rented apartment she slumped onto the edge of her bed and tried to gather her thoughts. She realised that she had been in danger and that God had looked after her. 'In the past when I needed help I often turned to father. I can't do that now - but I can turn to God. He knows how I miss my own dear father. I sometimes wish I had someone who I could really speak to about things… someone wise. But God knows my every need and all I really need is him.' With that she tried to go to sleep.

And though Amy never mentioned to the others in the family how much she really did miss her father everyone was really pleased when she told them about her new friend, Mr Robert Wilson. He was just the sort of friend she needed - older and wiser, someone who could help Amy and listen to her questions and problems. 'He's such a dear old man,' Amy smiled. 'A bit like a grandfather really. In fact I think I shall give him a nickname,' she announced. 'From now on we shall call him - the D.O.M. - which stands for the Dear Old Man. No other name will do for such a wonderful old gentleman like him.'

And wonderful he was for he really did his best to make sure that Amy and her family were looked after. He was a kind, elderly man who supported many Christian enterprises. He even owned a coalmine in the Lake District of England and Amy had some enjoyable holidays there. The D.O.M.'s house, The Grange, overlooked a beautiful valley and craggy mountains.

While staying there Amy could go for rides and breathe the clear country air. The D.O.M. was a widower with two sons still living at home. His only daughter had died when she was twenty-one, just the age Amy was now.

'You know I look on her like she was my own child,' the D.O.M. explained to Mrs. Carmichael one morning. 'And I'm concerned about Amy's health, as we all are. The work is too much for her. She is going to have to stop for her own sake. I would be honoured Mrs. Carmichael if you would allow Amy to live at my house. I am sure Amy will agree.'

Soon Mr. Wilson was reporting back to Amy's mother on the change in her. 'Amy is in good health again. Of course this means she is very busy too – you know what she is like. She has been asked to speak to children at Scripture Union meetings. They really enjoy these and I'm told there isn't a sound while she's speaking. She invites girls to the house where she runs games and a Bible Class, finishing up with that tasty gingerbread she makes for everyone.'

The D.O.M. treated Amy like a daughter and she was a loving companion to him. Amy's friends and family were pleased she was so well and that all was quiet and normal for her. However, one snowy evening in January 1892, all that changed abruptly. Amy was sitting on her own, going through her Ask and Receive book. She was stunned to hear God calling her to serve him as a missionary. The words 'Go, ye' that Jesus spoke to his disciples, sounded in her head. These words urged her towards a dramatic change.

Right after this other thoughts rushed in. If she went abroad now, what would happen to her mother and the D.O.M.? She knew she could live without the comforts and beautiful views at The Grange. A hard way of life working in large cities had shown her she could bear anything if she was working for God. 'But won't the D.O.M be lonely without me? And I should really stay to help mother too. I am not sure if my health will be strong enough to travel abroad and how will I have money to live on? Oh all these questions - I just don't know - how can I tell if this is just one of my ideas or a plan of God's?'

As the days passed, Amy knew it wasn't just her idea. At last she confided in her mother. Her letter began:

My Precious Mother,

Have you given your child unreservedly to the Lord for whatever he wills? As you know, for a long time the thought of those dying in the dark has been very present with me. I long to go to tell them of Jesus. Everything seems to be saying 'Go'... to those people who have no chance of hearing of the love which makes our lives so bright. But home claims seem to say 'stay'.

Yesterday I had a good talk with the D.O.M. I feel as if I am stabbing those I love. Many problems have risen in my mind, but trust leaves all results to God. I know very few of our friends will think I am right.

Two days later came her mother's welcome reply. What a help and support it was to read her words.

Yes, dearest Amy, God has lent you to me all these years as my strength, comfort and joy. When he asks you to go away, how can I say no? You are his, to take you where he pleases. I feel for our D.O.M. but God cannot make a mistake. 'The Lord is our Shepherd.'

After that the letters flew daily between Amy and her mother. She knew her call to be a genuine one but the place to go to had not been included. Amy remembered hearing Hudson Taylor in Belfast, speaking of millions of Chinese dying 'Saviourless, hopeless.' She decided to apply to the China Inland Mission. The D.O.M. took her to London for interviews. Suddenly everything came to a halt: the doctor could not pass Amy as fit enough to go to China. She returned to life at The Grange. Great patience was needed for the wait that followed. She carried on with her meetings, her riding and long walks with her terrier, Scamp.

Happy as the D.O.M. was to have her back home, he knew Amy was still searching for a clear instruction on where to go. One day, a whole year after that call of 'Go', she told him she knew. 'I must not just settle down here forever. I have a strange feeling I should go to Japan.'

'I know Mr Buxton, a missionary who is working there,' he told her, 'I can ask him to arrange to get you there, if you are sure.'

Was Amy sure? She knew only that she had to obey and become a missionary. Arrangements were made for her to travel by ship, first to Sri Lanka, and then on to China. Here she would wait for definite news about going to Japan.

Sri Lanka, China, Hong-Kong, India

Amy had always been a good sailor, so she really enjoyed the first part of the journey, even the storms. In Sri Lanka she met some old friends who were missionaries there. These friends actually asked her to stay to work with them but, by now, she felt sure she had a call to Japan. The next ship, to Shanghai, was smaller and badly run. Her cabin was infested by rats and cockroaches, so she and some other ladies slept on deck.

Amy then had a short stay in Shanghai and then, finally, took a ship for Japan. Here a typhoon made landing impossible. Instead, the captain put Amy and some very seasick Japanese into a little steam-tug. As she put her luggage ashore she looked around her through the driving rain. The busy port was teeming with people calling out to one another in a language unknown to her.

'Mr Buxton must be here surely? But I can't see him.' Amy was slightly concerned but tried to reassure herself. 'He'll be here shortly, I'll just have to be patient.' But as she waited and waited there was no sign of the elusive Mr. Buxton. 'I was told that he would be here to meet me,' Amy muttered, slightly annoyed. 'He's the one who is supposed to take me to the mission station. If he doesn't turn up then what will I do?' Amy sighed. People were beginning to look and stare at her. After Amy felt as though she had been waiting for hours a kindly Japanese woman came up and persuaded Amy to follow her. Eventually Amy was put in a rickshaw and sent to the only person they could think of who might help her – another white person - an American who was working as a trader in Japan.

'Well Miss Carmichael, you can't really stay with me but I do know of two lady missionaries who can take you in until Mr. Buxton arrives.'

Amy was more than a little relieved. The two lady missionaries generously took her in and a few days later Mr Buxton finally managed to complete his journey and Amy was now on her way to the mission station.

After so many weeks of travelling among strangers Amy was delighted at the warm welcome she received. The other missionaries clearly looked on her as a new member of their Christian family in Japan. Amy was grateful for this kindness so far from her home. Another source of delight to her was the scenery. There were two lakes and a castle built on a steep hill. Amy's bedroom gave her a beautiful view of the mountains. It reminded Amy just a little bit of home. But despite these memories Amy didn't allow herself to feel too homesick. She was eager to begin her work.

And Amy's work meant meeting the Japanese people and sharing her faith with them. She already knew from that bewildering wait at the port how strange the language sounded. As the weeks went by and she

spent hours studying it, she found it very odd. To tell
someone she was hungry she had to say 'my honourable
inside is empty'. To say someone had died in Japanese
was 'he has honourably deigned to cease to become'.
One evening when she arrived at a small country hotel,
the owner happily told her about the dinner menu: 'a
chicken has deigned to cease to become'.

Fortunately for Amy she was given an interpreter,
a Japanese Christian girl called Misaki San. With her
Amy was soon able to visit people in the town and in
nearby villages. One very cold day they went to visit
an old lady. As Amy spoke she listened eagerly to the
story of one who died to take away her sins. Amy prayed
silently for her. The old lady had noticed her fur gloves
and reached forward to touch them. 'What are these?'
she asked. Her attention had been lost and it was hard
to return her mind to the gospel story.

'Did you see how my clothes took her mind off what
I was saying?' Amy asked Misaki San as they walked back
to the mission-station. 'I know now why Hudson Taylor[1]
wore the plait and gown of the Chinese people. I have
to change, too.' As soon as she got home Amy hung
up her English clothes and put on a kimono. She went
on wearing her own shoes and stockings and kept her
hair in the same way as before. The kimono, a length of
silk wrapped round her body and held by a sash, was a
much cooler way to dress in that usually hot climate.

---

[1] Read about Hudson Taylor in, *An Adventure Begins* by Catherine Mackenzie; and his wife, Maria Taylor in, *Ten girls who made a difference*, by Irene Howat.

Amy next made a dark-blue kimono and embroidered the words 'God is Love' on its border. This led to some lively talks with the people of the town.

At the missionaries' Sunday services Amy found more changes to cope with. No one wore a hat or shoes, and everyone sat on the floor, like the Japanese. Everything in the houses seemed to her to be made of paper – baskets, trays, dustpans and even walls and windows. By sliding the walls back large rooms could be made. Amy soon discovered that wetting the paper meant you could see through a wall. In letters home she was soon answering her mother's questions about food.

'At the mission-station we eat in a thoroughly English way. When travelling we eat Japanese food. This includes eggs young and old, raw fish, brown seaweed, leathery scraps floating about in some terribly fishy liquid, sea-slugs and rice. I've found that I don't mind all these things nearly as much as I was afraid I would. Still, when I have been travelling a lot by rickshaw or boat in terrible heat, I can feel too worn out to eat like that. Out of sight of my Japanese hosts, I take out some bread and tea of my own.'

After many struggles with the language Amy was, at last, able to speak a little at meetings in people's houses. Sometimes these meetings would get a bit disruptive as people often carried on with household chores and child care as she spoke. Mothers would undress children to rub them with oil. Smokers would tap their metal pipes loudly on the charcoal fireplaces.

The loud crashing of a gong might sound from a nearby temple while hideous idols could be seen on shelves all round the room. But despite all this, sometimes people understood what Amy was so urgently talking about. God opened their hearts and minds.

'All alone you have come and well we have understood,' said one lady to Amy at the end of a meeting. This remark encouraged Amy so much and she thanked God for it. Here, as at home, boys and girls crowded in to hear Amy tell them Bible stories. She always started their meetings with singing and soon had the children joining in. One young boy came back to see her with a remarkable story.

'My grandfather and I spoke a lot together about how your God answers prayer. Last week I had an important job to do. I delivered the boxes of little cakes to a wedding. Do you know guests are given a box each of small pink and white cakes? The worst thing happened and I tripped and dropped them. I'd be in such trouble if everyone had cakes in bits. I thought of your words and I stopped and prayed, "Please let none of the cakes be broken." I had to wait until the wedding ceremony was over. It felt like ages. Then it was time to give the guests their cakes. Not one of them was even cracked. I told my grandfather, "Now I know God hears prayer, because God heard me."'

It had been such a joy for Amy to hear the boy tell his story. When she set up a magic lantern[1], these children

---

[1] A machine that missionaries often used last century to show pictures or images to illustrate their talks.

were amazed to see large bright pictures suddenly appear on the wall. One day she overheard a little girl tell her friend, 'Tonight they are going to show their God to us.' This alarmed Amy as she did not want them to think Jesus was like their idols. Again, she talked about this to Misaki San, 'The Bible never tells us what Jesus looked like. Perhaps showing a picture of him will confuse these children. There's only one way out of this – I will not show pictures of Jesus any more.'

All the time Amy worked with these people, she was looking for a way to free them from their worship of idols. She longed for them to see how happy and free they could be if they believed in Jesus. One evening Amy and other missionaries managed to speak to three Buddhist monks getting ready for their evening worship. One man who was very interested was arranging flowers at the shrine where he worshipped his ancestors. Beside him was an idol covered in flowers. 'We can be saved by the death of Jesus and by his life in us today,' Amy told him.

The monk paused and thought, then said, 'What you say must be true. Buddha died. How can he help us then? He may say "Be good" but, being dead, he cannot give us the power to obey him. If we can be saved by the life of Jesus, we want to see it lived. Can you show it to us?' Amy felt the challenge in those words. Here in Japan, so far from her home, she knew she had to show the life of the Lord Jesus. She had to live it among these people for them to see. Just how hard it was to do this she told one of her friends in a letter:

'Don't imagine that by crossing the sea and landing on a foreign shore you break the bonds of sin and turn into an angel. There is no romance in mission-work. There's no halo adorning us. I cannot work here without your prayers. I need you as my prayer-warrior, to share the battle with me.'

She soon found herself praying often for a village she really loved. There were eight Japanese Christians there. Amy believed it would strengthen the believers if they burnt their idols.

'Misaki San, you know I spent all yesterday praying about that village. I believe God will convert one person if we go there today.'

On their return she told the other missionaries how a young silk weaver had come to a true faith that day. A month later Amy told Misaki San that she had prayed for two converts. The silk weaver brought along her friend whom she had been telling of her new faith. This friend and an old lady became Christians that day. Two weeks later Amy believed, after prayer, that God would call four people. This visit was on her twenty-fifth birthday and Amy welcomed the four who became Christians on that day as special birthday gifts.

When she told the Christians in the village that she thought God would double the number again, they began to doubt. 'To ask for eight 'Jesus-persons' here is too much. You can't expect conversions every time.

To pray for things and not get them would be a very bad happening. It's best not to risk a disappointment.' They were all pleased, though, when Amy's faith was rewarded by seeing eight Buddhists give up their idols on that visit.

All this was at great cost to Amy. While speaking in the village she suffered a lot of pain in her face. When she returned to the mission-station she had to give in and lie still on her bed for several days.

Once she was up and about again she found out there were factory girls living in a poor part of the town. On her first visit there a crowd of boys jeered and threw stones at her. She had not given in when this happened in Belfast and Manchester, so she carried on the visits. By the end of her first year in Japan, eighty girls were coming to her meetings.

Even after twelve months Amy was still finding the Japanese language hard to master. A simple comment such as 'I like fine weather better than wet' in Japanese became 'Rain of coming down bad honourable weather than even good honourable weather of days of side good is.' Misaki San was a patient teacher but, when she gave Amy a word to spell using twenty-eight letters, her pupil felt she could do no more. 'I shall never, never, never, learn Japanese. You may put it on my tombstone: expired in despair' was Amy's final verdict.

Despite frequent aching in her face and headaches she kept on with her travelling and teaching. One extremely hot day she alarmed the Japanese Christians she visited by fainting. Back once more at the mission-station Amy had to be examined by the doctor. He had seen before the dreadful effect working in this climate had on her. After days of lying down helpless, she was often blind for hours afterwards. He knew how severe the illness they called 'Japanese head' could be, so he told her she should go to a resort in China for a long rest.

Leaving Japan in this way made Amy feel she was 'giving in.' On board ship for Shanghai she found a note from Misaki San, 'I know you will miss me, but Christ is sitting by you now, so please talk with him to forget me.' During the voyage she still suffered from the heat and had dreadful headaches. Fierce storms in the south China seas made her, for once, very seasick. When she arrived in Shanghai the missionaries saw how thin and ill she had become.

With their kindness and help Amy had a week of quiet rest in a room of her own. There she hung family photos and wrote letters home. Soon, though, she was praying for God to show her where she should go next. The answer came clearly, 'Go to Sri Lanka.' She remembered how her friends there had asked her to work with them so she wrote to tell them she was coming. The missionaries in Shanghai were horrified as they did not think she was well enough yet to travel so far on her own. Happily, someone else was travelling there too, so could look after her on board.

On reaching Hong Kong, Amy was struck down by an awful fever which made her feel very weak. 'What if I never reach Sri Lanka?' she thought, 'What if God's will for me is to give up and go home? How the Devil comes with doubts and fears.'

At last she was well enough to continue her journey. This time she stepped ashore in Sri Lanka to a very warm welcome from her friends. Though still tired and weak, she was pleased to find work for her to do. A missionary and his wife had died of fever, leaving a small group of women to run the mission-station. She moved into their thatch-roofed hut, soon got used to living on a mud floor and began teaching Bible stories to the local people.

A letter from her D.O.M. caused her great sadness. He wrote to warn her that her sudden move from Japan to Sri Lanka had upset the organisation which supported her financially. They had expected to be asked or, at least, told of this sudden change. A devastated Amy wrote at once, 'How could I wait and hesitate when God said, "Go forward." But I should have let it be known at home first. I see my wrongness, and cannot be sorry enough.'

Amy needed great patience in visiting people in the jungle villages. She told her mother in a letter:

'You go to a hut and find nobody in, you go to the next and find nobody wants you. You go the next and an old woman says, "Yes, you can talk if you like," and half-listens. Perhaps more drift in and you go on talking. It is so disappointing sometimes. Just when you think a heart seems touched by the wonderful story of Calvary, you get a

question about Buddhists not eating pigs or eggs like us and triviality takes over instead.'

The dark side of Buddhism appalled Amy. When a woman living near them was ill a devil-dance took place. Loud drumming and yelling went on all night. Three altars were set up and covered in water-lilies and candles. Amy was told it was risky for a woman on her own to visit Buddhist priests, but she did it. One asked her, 'You Christians believe God leads people who are seriously seeking the truth. Buddha was very serious, so why did he not find the truth?'

With questions like this Amy could only pray that God would help her to share his truth. It was a struggle and a challenge but with children Amy's cheerful, loving ways soon drew large numbers to her meetings. She needed an interpreter again as she was now learning yet another new language.

But it was more than language worries that Amy had to cope with. One evening a young woman rushed into Amy's hut, her face flushed and her breath laboured. Amy had just been studying some grammar lessons with her new interpreter. Both women were astonished when the young girl started yelling, 'He's got a knife! Stay inside!'

'Who has a knife?' Amy asked, puzzled.

'Lotus' husband!'

It was all the explanation that Amy needed. 'I knew there might be trouble when Lotus became a Christian. Lotus has a husband with a quick temper,' Amy explained.

'And he isn't pleased with you!' The young girl gasped. 'Look, he is coming towards the door waving a large carving knife. He blames you for converting Lotus to Christianity.'

All three women felt very afraid. There was only one thing to do. They knelt down and began praying. Amy found it very hard to keep her eyes shut. They heard the noise of someone coming into their hut but went on praying aloud. Amy did not look to see what their would-be attacker was doing. When, at last, she opened her eyes she saw him holding his knife over their heads. They all kept still but looked up at him. He changed his mind and moved away. More long prayers followed, of thanks to God for their escape.

Amy wiped the sweat off her brow, 'With all this heat and hot-headed husbands, a jungle life is a hard life indeed,' she muttered to herself.

But with Amy's love of flowers and trees she actually found many things in the jungle to enjoy. She had a peaceful few minutes one day watching a bird called a honey-sucker. It was small and bright blue. As it hovered by a large white flower it dipped its curved beak into the fragrant blossom.

'Is this to be the place,' Amy wondered, 'where I can serve God?' When her mother suggested she should return home to recover fully she replied, 'It may be that God has only sent me here as a stopgap. Part of a soldier's duty is to fill gaps. Talk of coming home! Did ever a soldier, worth calling one, run away at the first shot! Praise the Lord – the pain is over and I am strong for the battle again. The doctor has said I must not return to the climate of Japan, but I may work in Sri Lanka. Now all is settled!'

Amy was relieved to be able to give her mother that good news. However, shattering news from home changed Amy's plans abruptly. The D.O.M. had had a stroke. She borrowed warm clothes from a missionary and sailed to London the next day. She arrived at The Grange by Christmas. Mr Wilson did gradually recover, helped partly by the return of his beloved Amy. He was overjoyed, even thinking she was back to stay. However the D.O.M. soon saw that this was not to be, as Amy was again searching for a place abroad to serve in.

A letter from a friend in Southern India told her that the climate there was healthy and pleasant. Amy was aware that doctors would ban her from hotter climates, yet she fretted that this place 'sounded much too easy.' The missionary society out there had a station and a hospital and her help would lighten the load for others. This was enough for Amy. She went to London for an interview, was accepted and parted from her D.O.M. soon after his seventieth birthday. In October 1895, Amy sailed to India.

Tinnevelly

Amy's friend was overjoyed to see her. 'You look as fresh as a daisy!' she exclaimed. But over the next few days Mrs Carr realised that her young friend wasn't as well as she looked. She was a nurse at the mission hospital so quickly realised that Amy was not well. In the three weeks Amy had spent at the port her ship docked at, she had caught a fever.

'I have a dreadful headache and such awful pain in my legs and arms,' Amy told her friend.

'That's why we call it "break-bone fever,"' she replied, 'It's the bite of the mosquito that causes it. It's a good thing you've come to work in a hospital as we can put you to bed and look after you through the worst of it.'

Amy had not expected to arrive like this. On her birthday just a few weeks later she lay in bed, utterly exhausted and aching all over. 'For the first time in my life I know what it is to wake up depressed, and feel low and wormy.'

By the new year, 1896, good nursing had helped her recover and she threw herself into her work with the Indian patients. As always with Amy, she worked hard and she played hard. In that tropical climate everyone was forced to rest for two hours around midday. In the evening coolness she could enjoy herself. She soon had a pony she called Laddie and quickly gained a reputation for her riding. One evening the British Area Ruler was astonished to find his carriage overtaken on his way home by a pony. In the speed and dust he could just make out a small female with flowing brown hair riding the pony. His wife soon put him in the picture. 'That's the new missionary at the hospital. Her name is Amy Carmichael but I've heard they call her "Madcap" for the unusual things she does.'

Such freedom meant a lot to Amy as her work was not always easy. One job was looking after the household accounts. This meant getting to know and handle Indian money. Much harder though, was tackling a new language, Tamil. Very soon Amy was admitting that, like Japanese, this was causing her to despair.

'There are 216 letters in the Tamil alphabet,' Amy sighed exasperated. 'And I know that there is only one solution to this - hard work!' So Amy spent six hours every day studying the language. She quickly became good friends with yet another interpreter, a Christian Indian woman named Saral. Their friendship was full of laughter at Amy's Tamil mistakes and full of fun as they went about their work together.

When the hottest months of April and May came, missionaries left the blistering hot plains and stayed at houses up in the hills. To Amy it seemed natural to take Saral with her. Someone paid her a visit to sort out what was going on.

'Are you seriously planning to take your Indian servant with you?' he asked

'Of course I am. She has called me the child of her heart. Why should she be left behind?'

'Well, at least she can sleep in the native quarters. This is a chance for us to be just British people on holiday together.'

'I intend to visit poor tribespeople up in the hills,' said Amy, 'I want Saral to share my room so that I can practise speaking Tamil'.

'Well, at least make her sleep on the floor. She'll be used to that,' was his only response. Amy had to give in and let Saral sleep in the native quarters.

But it annoyed Amy immensely and struck her as being highly unfair. Saral wasn't just a servant to her but a very close friend and co-worker. But everywhere Amy went she could see servants that were ill treated and despised by their masters. 'It's all to do with the Hindu caste system,' Amy realised. 'But the British do nothing to stop it. The Hindu caste system ensures that they have plenty of servants too.'

Saral explained the Hindu caste system to Amy one evening as they sat on the veranda in the cool breeze.

'If an Indian is born to a family in a certain caste he remains in that caste all his life and does only the work allowed to that caste. Cooking, dusting, laundry, gardening, sweeping and emptying the latrines are all done by Indian servants according to their low caste. Some castes are very high and aristocratic. But other castes are so low a high caste person will not even bring himself to touch them. They are despised. They are untouchables.'

Amy sighed in despair at the injustice of it all.

'How I long to be one with your country people, Saral. You are not untouchable - no one is. I long to live alongside you and speak your language. I long to tell you of the love of Jesus. How can Christians behave like they did on Sunday?'

Saral just shrugged her shoulders but Amy stamped her foot.

'The British governor and his family sat at the front of the church, but you and the other Indian Christians had to sit at the back. This is not what Jesus told us to be like.'

But the summer months were not all disappointment for Amy. She met a missionary she had already heard a lot of talk about, Thomas Walker.

Mr and Mrs Walker had been working in India for eleven years in an area known as Tinnevelly, about three hundred miles south of Bangalore. When Amy told him about her problems in learning Tamil, he told her of his own struggles with the language. 'Visit us at Tinnevelly and I will help you to learn Tamil,' Mr Walker urged.

Amy immediately accepted his invitation and soon became firm friends with him and his wife. Mr Walker was planning a mission to the many local villages and, once Amy had passed her Tamil exam, he asked the Bangalore hospital to allow Amy to come and work with the Walkers full time. Amy was excited at the chance of working with the villagers at last. The night before she was due to leave she went for a moonlight drive with a friend. Amy spotted a dark shadow ahead of them and grabbed the reins sharply from her friend's hands. They turned the horse just in time: they had nearly driven straight into a deep ditch. The next morning the Bible verse in Amy's daily reading was, 'My Presence will go with you.'

Amy smiled. She knew a little of what was ahead of her. With only a tent to stay in, it would be hard work but rewarding. And the work was partly helped, partly hindered by travelling around in a bandy, a springless two-wheeled cart. Amy wrote home:

'When at last I settled down to slumber, Saral rolled over on top of me, bumping me black and blue. It is, except for the Chinese wheelbarrow, the most tiring way of going about I ever came across.'

They travelled by night to escape the heat but the jerking of the wheels on the rutted roads made sleep difficult. Amy was soon suffering the terrible face pain of neuralgia again. They were all delighted when friends in England sent a large tent so that they could have longer stays in each village.

But the longer village stays made Amy conscious of her dress style once more. 'I wore a Kimono in Japan,' she remembered. 'I think I should now wear a sari. It will help me get alongside the Indian people. Perhaps it will make speaking to them a little bit easier too,' she hoped. However, Amy often found talking to the villagers remained an unpleasant, or even alarming, experience. Their habit of chewing betel-leaf juice blackened their teeth and made their mouths bright red. Two boys from a high caste told Amy that if they believed what she was telling them, they would be beaten to death.

With stories like that, Amy could hardly believe that she was living in such a beautiful area. Tinnevelly was from a Tamil name meaning 'Hedge of the Holy Paddy Field'. After the monsoon the young rice growing in the paddy fields became a shining green sea.

Amy soon found out that the two boys who spoke to her of revenge on Christian converts had not been making up a story. Very early one morning she was woken up by shouts outside The Walkers' bungalow.

'Refuge! Refuge!' a girl was calling. Amy dashed outside and saw a girl of about seventeen standing there. They went inside and she told her story to Amy and the Walkers.

'I went to the mission school in Great Lake village. A lady there gave me a Bible because I told her I trusted in the Lord Jesus. I had to keep this a secret because I am from a high caste. I let my elder brother smear the ashes sacred to Hindus on my forehead. When he had gone I rubbed them off again. My family were angry with me so for three years I was like a prisoner. This morning I took a risk and left my home. Please help me.'

As she finished speaking, everyone heard a lot of noise on the veranda. She looked outside and called out, 'Those people are my family. They have come to fetch me home. Please let me stay with you and live as a Christian.'

Her brother, the head of the family, now stepped forward. 'Come back to us. We are your own people. You cannot give up our religion.'

Her mother also began begging her to return. 'You must not break caste by living with these white people. We will let you go to church. We will not force you to marry. Please come back or we will live in shame.'

The girl was trembling and looked anxious. 'I cannot go back,' she declared.

Thomas stepped forward. 'You have done your best to change her mind. She has refused. You have heard her. She is free to go or stay.'

At this the family left. That night the mission school was burnt down. A threat was made that poison would be thrown in the girl's face if she went to church. Amy took her to another mission house further away. A few months later she asked for baptism and took a new name for her new life, Jewels of Victory.

Everyone now fully realised the danger they were facing. Amy and the Walkers knew they had to go on with their work, so prayed for more Indian workers to travel to the villages. But the Indian people, even the Christians sometimes, resented Amy and her work.

The Woman who runs
like a Hare

'That woman who runs like the hare has tricked us all into foolishness,' an old man told his neighbours. The people knew that he meant Amy. They also knew that he belonged to the local Christian church but treated his daughter-in-law, Ponnammal, as a household drudge. Ponnammal's husband, his son, had died, so she and her little girl still lived with him. But now she had become a Christian and Amy recruited her for the team of village workers. It was an answer to Amy's prayer for more Indian workers but Ponnammal's father-in-law was more than a little annoyed at losing his household help.

Another widow, who took the name of Blessing when she became a believer, joined Amy in a visit to a rather argumentative woman. 'You're ignorant, just a block of wood! I can read and quote poetry,' the rather pompous woman boasted to Blessing.

Amy was thrilled to hear her reply, 'I am a believer for one month only. I have no wisdom to answer you, but I can read this book of God. In my heart His peace and joy are dwelling. Is not joy better than learning?'

And as Amy went around the villages with two Christian widows, other local women assumed she too had been widowed. One old lady grabbed her own hair, then pointed to Amy's and demanded, 'Are you a widow? You have no oil on your hair so you must be. Or can't you even afford a half penny a month to buy good oil?'

Amy often found these little misunderstandings an amusing element of her day but there were discouragements too. One day, as Amy and some workers approached a temple fort, villagers came out to pelt them with ashes, smearing Amy's hair and the lemon-coloured sari that she wore. On another occasion a Hindu devil-dancer yelled at them, 'Go away. If I come to your god my devil-god will kill me. Tell your lies somewhere else.' An old man called out, 'Who wants your Jesus here?' Even some of the so-called Christian Indians argued against Amy. 'You say a Christian should not quarrel, but I love a good fight. If I am converted I have to forgive people and I know a woman I'll never forgive.' However, Amy and her team did not give up.

One boy told Amy a particular story of how God had helped him. 'I asked my father for help with my sin. Your teaching showed me my burden of sin was heavy. He told me to learn the Thousand Verses of our religion and my sin would melt away. It made no difference. Then my father told me to wait a year and see if I found a way to get rid of my sin. But I heard Christians singing the words, "Jesus is calling." The next morning I came here and found that Jesus. Now my burden of sin has gone like the dew when it sees the sun!'

Amy loved to hear how God was working with these people, but when a Hindu converted to Christianity Amy knew that it could cause the convert and the mission severe problems.

When the first convert girl left her Hindu home to be baptised this caused a great commotion. Amy and the other workers were pelted with handfuls of refuse and chased out of all the villages near the one the girl had lived in. As a result Amy and the others had to move to another village. It didn't take them long to start up their gospel meetings again and it was at one of those meetings that a girl of eleven heard about the God who could change her quick temper. She noticed Amy, in her sari as usual, and felt drawn to her friendly face and ways. 'If only I could go to her, she would have a place in her heart for me.' The girl was called Arulai.

However, Arulai's parents tried their best to put a stop to her interest in the Christian meetings. They took her to a temple of the god Siva but Arulai was not taken in by the worship there.

'These are dead idols. All the garlands and jewels here have no life behind them,' she said to herself.

As her family thought she was bewitched by Amy, they sent Arulai to live with an uncle in another village. This uncle never thought to tell his relations that his village was actually very close to one of the mission stations. Arulai was overjoyed one Sunday to see Amy sitting on the floor of the church. After the service Arulai went to the mission compound and spent much time with Amy learning more about the Lord Jesus.

When her parents heard of this they immediately removed her from her uncle's home. For months Amy heard nothing more of Arulai. Rumours reached her that the young girl had gone back on her new faith. As Amy carried on with her work she had to struggle with other children and converts who were persecuted for their faith. Still there was no sign of Arulai, and Amy feared the worst.

Then, one night, eight months later, there came a sound at the bungalow door and Arulai slipped into the room. She was very ill and it took Amy's constant care to bring her back to good health. Arulai's father was impressed by the care given to his daughter but still wanted to take her home. Amy heard Arulai praying last thing at night, 'Don't let me go back to the dark, please, Lord. Let me live in the light.'

Amy sighed - the night was a very frightening place to be without Jesus, without love, without hope of heaven. Amy soothed young Arulai's anxious dreams with a gentle song of Christ's love. Amy knew now that God had led her to India to reach out to the children with the love of Jesus. Yet she also knew there were many in need who were hidden away from the eyes of foreigners. Would she ever be able to reach those children as well?

Pearl-eyes and the
Child Stealer

'I couldn't wait any longer. I'm sorry. I know how you love your early morning cup of tea and your prayer-time.' Amy hardly heard all these apologies from Ponnammal because she was too interested in looking at the sad-faced little girl clutching her friend's hand. In her turn, the girl stared back at Amy, amazed at her first sight of a white-faced foreigner.

'She just turned up outside the church yesterday. It was too late to find where she lived, so I took her home with me for the night. She keeps saying she wants to see you. I'm afraid she calls you by your name in the villages, "the child-stealing Amma".'

'I'm used to that by now. Don't worry. I rather like the "Amma" part of it, as I do feel like a mother to the children we care for here. Now, little one, come here to me.'

The little girl at once ran to Amy and climbed up on her lap. 'My name is Pearl-eyes and I want to stay here always. I have come to stay.'

Amy held her and kissed her before daring to ask any personal questions.

'Will you tell me where you have come from?' asked Amy gently.

'I have run away from the temple-women's house at Great Lake village. They warned us all about you, Amma. Everything was horrid in the temple, dark and stern. They were cruel to me, so you couldn't be worse. I thought I'd risk coming here to you.'

'Let's go into the bungalow so you can have a meal. You've walked a long way by yourself. You must have crossed the stream and walked through woods. What a brave girl you are,' said Amy.

'Oh, I've done much more dangerous things,' boasted the little girl. She felt safe now so looked much happier. She chattered to Amy as she poured her some milk.

'Oh, Pearl-eyes, what made those terrible burns on your hands?' Amy exclaimed.

'Oh, that's what the temple-women did to me. I tried running away from them before. I walked miles and miles to get back home to my mother. That was a dangerous journey but I did it. It was lovely to be back with my mother, in my own village. But the temple-women followed me and my mother gave me back to them. They were very angry with me. At their house they burnt my hands with hot irons. They said the marks would stop anyone from helping me to escape because they would see I belonged to the god. I am seven years old now and will soon be taken to the temple to live there forever. I don't want to do that.'

Amy's eyes filled with tears and she hugged the little girl to her. The next day the temple-women arrived at the bungalow. 'Have you any proof to show us that she is yours?' asked Thomas Walker.

'We've no papers for her, if that's what you mean, but she belongs with us.'

'Pearl-eyes, do you want to go and live with these people?' Thomas asked.

'No, I won't go with them!' shouted Pearl-eyes.

The women knew they were defeated and left.

'It's so horrible that little girls are taken away from their homes like this. Are there many of them working in temples, Ponnammal?' asked Amy later that night.

'I've heard of this happening but it is kept secret. In those temple compounds no one can really see what is going on. My father-in-law made me do all his work but, at least, my daughter and I had somewhere to live. For many widows giving or selling a child to the priest is the only way to get money to survive.'

'I can't believe that our British rulers do nothing about it. I must do something,' said Amy.

'Oh, Amma,' protested Ponnammal, 'you are so busy already, how can you do more? I will do my best to help you, but how do we know where to start?'

'We travel to teach in many of the villages,' said Amy. 'There are four temples, at least, in this area. If we keep our eyes and ears open, sooner or later we will find out where temple-women have their houses. When a widow is very poor we can help her and keep watch over her family. Now I have seen Pearl-eyes I know I have to find more temple-children and set them free.'

'Do you realise that, if Pearl-eyes had reached the church earlier I would have found out where she lived. I would have taken her back to them not knowing they were temple-women,' said an anxious Ponnammal.

'If Pearl-eyes had made her escape last week we would have been fifty miles away from here,' said Amy. 'Somehow it seems God timed it all perfectly.'

And it wasn't only timing that God planned perfectly. Over and over again he provided for the needs of the little missionary team. Even though their accommodation was an old, leaky, abandoned mission house - it was a base and it was theirs. To begin with it was just somewhere to stay between long visits to the villages. But as more converts came to stay, further work had to be done to make it homely for the children. Yet no more temple girls were discovered and brought there.

Three years after Pearl-eyes came to Amy a minister who knew of Amy's search came to see her. 'I know you have been trying to find girls given to the temple-women. I have a baby with me. I heard she had been given to them as soon as she was born. I was able to rescue her. She's only two weeks old now.'

Amy took the baby in her arms. 'Pearl-eyes, you may give her a name,' Amy told her.

'Amethyst, a jewel from the Holy City,' said Pearl-eyes.

The same minister brought another baby. Six more temple girls were rescued that year. More people were willing to tell where these girls and babies were. As the bungalow filled up and Amy became busy feeding and nursing the children, she faced a challenge in her way of life.

'Can it be right,' she thought, 'for us to turn from the village work and become just nursemaids?' As the number of children reached seventeen Amy turned to her Bible for answers. She read again how Jesus took up a towel and washed his disciples' feet before his last Passover supper with them. 'Only our wise God knows which work is unimportant and which is worth doing. Rescuing babies is truly a venture of faith,' she decided.

And there were lots of things that Amy required faith for. One was the ever increasing needs for Amy's growing family. The mission-compound was part of a jungle village called Dohnavur. One thing in its favour was its position. There were mountains to the west of the village and it was free of the mosquitoes that carried malaria. Yet water was needed. Not that water was scarce. The land provided wells with a plentiful supply, but some improvements such as wells and fresh clean water could not be done without money. Amy's energetic efforts soon brought about improvements.

Amy herself received money regularly from the D.O.M. to support her work in India. 'I am going to sell my pony,' Amy decided one day. 'I enjoy riding him but it means I am on my own. When I travel I feel I should be with everyone else in the bandy cart'.

'I have been praying that we can build a nursery for all our babies,' Ponnammal told her.

'We will go ahead with that soon,' replied Amy, 'I am sure God will give us the money we need.'

'Yes, earthen floors and a thatched roof can be made in the village, but sun-dried bricks must be bought,' Ponnnammal agreed.

Amy nodded, she knew that too and she knew that God would provide. So it was a surprise and it wasn't a surprise when the next post arrived. A friend at home had sent a letter with a gift of money – the exact amount needed to pay for the bricks. Soon after this an anonymous gift of money arrived with a note, 'For the nursery.' Then just at this time, when so much extra money was needed, another emergency arose.

Ponnammal rushed into Amy's room one morning with urgent news. 'A little girl, only eight years old, is going to be sold to the temple-women by her father. He has told me he will hand her over to you for one hundred rupees.'

In her prayers that night Amy searched for the right decision. 'I must rescue her. But if people find out I will bid for her against the temple-women, things will become impossible. If I go ahead and pay the money how can I be sure that it is God's will and not just me doing what I want?'

'I feel it will be a mistake to pay money for her,' was Ponnammal's advice the next day. Amy, though, had an idea. 'I have asked God to send us a gift of one hundred rupees. That's more than any single gift we've ever received.'

Ten days later a cheque for that amount arrived from another missionary. Amy paid it to the girl's father. First, though, the cheque was placed on the floor and Amy gathered together all the workers in the nursery. They knelt down and thanked their Heavenly Father for his kindness and generosity.

Ponnammal smiled and said to the other workers. 'God has answered our prayer quicker than Amy can run.' And the local people were quite right to describe Amy's speed of movement as like that of a hare. Not everyone could keep up with her. She used to tease Blessing about this. 'Are you an elephant that you walk so slowly?' Amy asked her. With so many children to look after it was a good thing Amy could move swiftly from one need to another. When she was with a child, however, no one would have thought there was any need for hurry at all. She gave them all her full attention and love.

However, Amy knew her limitations. 'We need more workers - nurses and other helpers from England. When the babies fall ill we have to take them to the missionary hospital in a bullock cart, and that takes us a day and a half.'

'I know,' Ponnammal sighed. 'And with the road so unsafe the journey is treacherous. I still shake when I remember the hurricane. When it struck us it overturned the carts. We were all terrified - especially the babies.'

'Thankfully no bones were broken,' Amy added. 'But I do need to get out my ask and receive book again. I shall ask God for more helpers and more converts.'

One very definite answer to Amy's prayer was the baptism, early in 1907, of seven Dohnavur girls.

Amma

'What have you been getting up to? I didn't expect to see babies and little girls everywhere when I returned.' Thomas Walker was standing looking amazed at the sight of so many cradles and the squealing brown bundles tucked up inside them. He and his wife had just been on a visit to England. 'If my wife could only see this, she would be thrilled that you have rescued more temple babies.'

'I hope she'll be well enough to travel back to us soon,' said Amy. 'We found some of these children ourselves. I even stayed in a hostel for pilgrims and priests. I kept a sharp watch for any clues about where temple women were living. Ponnammal and I found one child when we were spending the night in a cow-barn. That was hard for you, Ponnammal, wasn't it?'

Ponnammal grimaced slightly, 'I try to live in a new way now, but my caste thinks it's dreadful to sleep in such a place. But Jesus was humble and was born in a Bethlehem stable. That makes it all right for me,' she replied, 'and because we were there we heard through the thin wall someone in the house talking about a plan to put a girl in the temple. He even said where she lived so we went straight there the next day and rescued her.' And as a little toddler got herself tangled

73

up in Amy's sari she laughed out loud, 'I'm certainly finding out how true the Tamil proverb is, "Children tie the mother's feet." I believe God wants me to stay here and bring up these children.'

'But, Amy, are you putting yourself in too much danger when searching for them?' Thomas asked her.

'I never go alone and I dress to fit in with other women. I even stain my face and arms with coffee to avoid being noticed. Thanks to you my Tamil speech is accepted by the Indians,' she replied. 'To all appearances I'm just like one of the locals. My own mother wouldn't recognise me sometimes.'

And in 1905 Amy's mother was certainly surprised to see her daughter looking after sick children, bathing and feeding babies and even punishing them when they were really badly-behaved. 'I can see why everyone here calls you Amma, you really are a mother to them all,' she told her daughter.

'And I am so glad to see you … my mother,' Amy replied. 'It's lovely to have you here … and for such a nice long stay too.'

'I've been looking forward to it also,' Mrs Carmichael agreed. 'It has been fascinating to hear all your stories by letter - but it's even better to hear you tell them to me in person. To think that all these children have been rescued from a life of misery in the temples! One of the mission workers told me the other day about a baby she brought from Bangalore.'

'Yes, that's right,' Amy remembered. 'The baby was from the Brahman caste. They are a caste or group of people that are of noble birth. Because they could see that our worker was not of a high-caste, she was accused of kidnapping the baby. When the train stopped a Brahman official inspected the child. 'She isn't yours!' he shouted and people started yelling for them both to be pulled off the train. Just at that moment the train began to move and the official slammed the door. We are so thankful to God that she and the baby got away!'

One day Mrs Carmichael became interested in watching a little girl carrying a bowl of water for the flowers Amy had planted to brighten up the compound. Ponnammal offered to tell Mrs Carmichael the story of this little girl's arrival. 'When she was only a tiny baby her father left her mother, so they lived with her grandmother. They were a low caste and very poor. Neighbours who felt sorry for the mother told her to sell the baby to the temple priests. The mother was tempted, but she knew how cruel this was so, instead, she set out to find her husband. She went to a great temple sacred to Siva and gave an offering of fruit and a little money to the priests. She then flung herself down on her face before the idol. No one could tell her where her husband was. Then the little one fell ill. Her mother found a nurse who agreed to take care of the baby and bring her up as her own. She even promised never to sell the child to work in the temple. Soon after that one of our workers heard she had done that very thing. We rescued her from the temple women and brought her here.'

'What a wonderful story,' Mrs Carmichael exclaimed. 'And I can see how busy you all are with these children. In fact … you are so busy I'm sure you could do with a little help. I don't have much to offer but I could teach the girls to sew a little and to speak English.'

Amy jumped at the idea and very soon Amy's mother was also as busy as the rest of the team. Mrs Carmichael knew how keen her family were to know more about their sister so she wrote home as often as she could:

Dear Children,

Amy never thinks of herself till all is done. I'm so glad to have been with her, if only to make sure she sits down and eats some food now and then. I'm sure she has little sleep. If she hears a child cry out in the night she runs over to see to her. An Indian cradle is a hammock, a long strip of white cloth knotted to a rope thrown over a beam in the ceiling. I have been helping to sew tapes across the cloth to make it safer. Amy has told me how one night she woke up, yet could hear no crying. It seemed there was no reason to go across to the nursery and yet she felt disturbed. She went in, just in time to rescue a six-month-old baby who had somehow pushed her head between the tapes. She was being strangled so could not cry out.

I am so grateful that Amy has such a good friend as Ponnammal working with her. She is not physically strong but is truly the Lord's. She is so kind and so wise. She even has the most ill baby in her own bedroom at night in case help is needed. She is just like my Amy in the way she pours herself out to serve the children.'

When news reached Amy of the D.O.M.'s death, what a comfort it was to her to have her mother to turn to.

'Despite how the D.O.M. felt and how I felt at your leaving us, there is no doubt in my mind that you are where God wants you to be,' Mrs Carmichael comforted Amy. 'You chatter away in Tamil as fast as all the Indian women. You could almost be one of them, wearing that sari.'

'Oh, mother, you've just made me remember something very important. Do you recall how I kept on when I was little about having blue eyes like you?'

'Yes, and because I told you God always answers prayer you thought you could get rid of your brown eyes and have them turned into blue. You were only three at the time,' answered her mother.

'I knelt by my bed one night and asked God to turn my brown eyes blue. I felt so excited in the morning, climbing up on a chair to look in the mirror. It was such a let-down to see they were still brown. I think it was either you or Dad who explained that God sometimes says "no" to our prayers and that his decisions are for our good. When I've been out searching for temple children, blue eyes would have been a giveaway that I was a foreigner. God always knows what is best for us.'

The sad day came when Mrs Carmichael had to return to England. Amy missed her advice and companionship but, without knowing it, she had sent home an ambassador for the mission at Dohnavur. Amy's mother had been so impressed by the atmosphere of love and obedience at Dohnavur she just had to tell people. 'There was never an angry look or an impatient word among them. All were so loving and unselfish,' Mrs Carmichael said to everyone she met.

However, frequent illness, and sometimes death of babies in her care troubled Amy. She began to pray that a children's nurse would volunteer to come to them. A young woman did come but stayed only a few months before leaving to marry a man she had met on board ship. It was hard to accept that answer to prayer.

Some months after Mrs Carmichael went home, a cholera epidemic struck the villages near the compound. Amy and the Indian workers visited the sick but had no doctor to guide them and little medicine of any kind. Thankfully not one of the children had cholera, despite their own carers' being in daily contact with it.

It was not long before the British rulers of that part of South India began to find fault with Amy and her home for the children. She had to bring this out into the open, so talked it over with Mr and Mrs Walker. Amy asked them what exactly it was that people were saying about her.

'A lot of it's just plain preposterous,' he said, 'saying your efforts to save temple children is just a stunt, to draw attention to yourself. The British view is that, as the temple system is centuries old, it's best to leave well alone. If only they'd seen some of the children we have!'

'They just don't want to understand,' Mrs Walker added, 'They disapprove of you wearing saris and doing work that is beneath a white woman.'

Happily for Amy, friends in England saw things differently. More wanted to help support her work. Amy had never directly asked for money for her work. She only asked her Heavenly Father for the needs of the children. When termites began tunnelling up the walls of the old nurseries, the workers spread cow dung onto the mud floors to harden the surface. As more gifts of money came to Dohnavur Amy had to decide if she should buy more lasting but expensive materials. Her common sense led her to re-build with burnt bricks and tiled roofs and floors.

One day when she was in the middle of supervising some tiling, she couldn't help but smile at her situation. 'Here I am a mother, nurse, doctor, buildings overseer, financial manager and missionary and enjoying it thoroughly.'

Despite her many duties Amy never asked anyone to do a job she was not ready to do herself. No chore was beneath her. The women were often surprised to see Amy joining in. To see a white woman coming into the room with a cloth and brush was astonishing. But then Amy would soon be telling them stories, making them laugh so much they hardly noticed how hard they, and Amy herself, were working.

A Letter from a Queen

'There are too many of them. We'll never get out!' Amy and one of the missionary nurses were being pushed to the side of the road. A huge crowd of Indians were surging forward. Amy managed to step back into the porch of a house and pulled her colleague in after her. 'At least here we'll be out of the sun for a bit,' Amy laughed nervously. 'This is certainly turning out to be a lively morning,' said Amy. 'I thought we might hear of a temple girl if we came to this town today. However, I think we've got ourselves in the middle of one of their Hindu festivals.'

Amy was right. Just then hundreds of men, stripped to the waist, came into view. Their backs were glistening with sweat as they pulled on long, thick ropes. Behind them came a gigantic wooden cart, slowly rolling forward on large wheels. 'Whatever is that?' asked Amy's friend.

'We're in one of the Car festivals,' Amy explained. ' The people drag their idol to the temple. This is the Juggernaut, another name for Vishnu. I'm sorry to tell you that Vishnu means "Lord of the World." The men think it a great honour to pull the car or Juggernaut, all the way. Do you see those policemen over there? They're keeping watch because sometimes people will throw themselves under the car wheels. They think a death like that will please the god.' Amy shuddered.

She couldn't say any more as a terrible din began. Drums were banged loudly, cymbals clashed and a shrill piping sound added to the noise. The crowds were shouting out the slogans that told of their loyalty to Vishnu. At last the Juggernaut passed right in front of them. It was very dark and was covered in carvings of stories of the gods. Coloured streamers and tinsel decorated its sides. Garlands of flowers and palm branches hung down from the shrine at the very top.

It was then, looking upwards at the figure of the idol, that Amy saw the little boys. The youngest looked about five and the oldest perhaps nine. They clambered like monkeys up and down the sides of the Car, collecting baskets of flowers from the crowds. In front of the altar and the idol, on the very top, sat a small boy with a wreath of pink flowers over his bare shoulders.

Suddenly the Car jerked and came to a halt. A frenzy broke out amongst the men pulling it. 'The god will kill us for this. He will punish us all,' they shouted. Amy pulled her friend back as much as she could to be out of sight, for white women would be an easy target to blame for this hold-up. At last palm branches were brought to put under the wheels and the whole thing was got in motion again. It was followed by a naked devotee of the god rolling his body along the ground and holding his begging-bowl.

In her journal that night Amy wrote of how sad such a sight made her. 'Never has one ray of light come from the idols of the people, only a darkness which has defiled the mind of millions of India.'

It was just such an awful prospect. Amy wept when she remembered the little boy with the pink flowers over his shoulders. 'We need more workers Lord,' she prayed. 'You have sent some and we thank you for them - but we need more. Please send more.'

Amy's prayers for medical help were answered when a trained nurse, Mabel Wade, came out from Yorkshire to help at Dohnavur. But Mabel was not a doctor and when a doctor was needed it meant a day-and-a-half journey to the nearest hospital. Often this journey was just far too long for some of Amy's little patients.

When Lulla, a five-year-old Brahman child developed a dangerous illness, Mabel and Ponnammal did all they could for her. Amy, too, watched over her and, as Lulla struggled for breath, close to death, Amy prayed to the Lord to take her quickly. Suddenly a change came over the little girl. She looked up and clapped her hands. She flung her arms round Amy's neck, then round Mabel's and then Ponnammal's. She clapped her hands again and smiled happily at the three women, then sank back on the bed and drew her last breath. 'When Thomas returns, we must tell him how we saw little Lulla enter heaven. He was very fond of her and was showing her the microscope he gave us just before he left.'

Six days later a telegram arrived, telling Amy that Thomas Walker was dead. She had often told friends that she thought of him as an older brother. He had been a loyal friend whose advice and encouragement had been so valuable. As always, it was Ponnammal who gave Amy love and comfort in this terrible loss. She could also remind Amy of happy memories.

'Do you remember the squirrel? Poor Mr Walker certainly didn't share your great love of animals. You let that squirrel come to the breakfast-table. When Mr Walker came back from a trip, he was shocked to see the squirrel by his tea-cup the next morning. He shouted out, the squirrel jumped onto his shoulder, dashed across the table, upset the milk jug and landed in the butter. When you accused him of not liking animals he replied, "I do like them – but in their own place." He was fifty-three years old, a good age for an Indian, but not very old for an Englishman, I suppose.'

'He was a missionary who knew how to have fun,' Amy said. 'Do you remember when we had that trip to the seaside? Boatmen took us out for a sail. Their boat was just three logs tied together. Half a mile from shore a wave swept five of us into the sea. Somehow he helped to drag us all back on to the raft. He wanted to head for the shore but I wanted to go on and he let me. We were drenched but the sun soon dried us off and we all sang hymns in Tamil. I felt like a child again.'

Mrs Walker was still in England and sent Amy a telegram that included Job's words, 'The Lord gave and the Lord has taken away.' Within a week Amy had three offers of help.

Two women wrote to Amy 'When we heard that Thomas had died we both realised it was God's plan for us to come to Dohnavur.' Both women were trained teachers so were able to take over the children's education.

'This is wonderful,' Amy hugged herself in glee. 'How good God is to me. These women have been sent by him. In the past I have tried to teach the children a love of Creation. I sometimes took a group out in the early morning to look up at the stars. They even named their dolls after them. When the new nursery was being built I took some of them to see it. We made a game of naming the stones after the mountains of Africa. They will learn so much more from the new teachers and I will have time to deal with other work.'

A young Indian man, Arul Dasan, who had worked for Thomas Walker, offered to come to Dohnavur, too. 'I will sort out all the building work for you,' he told Amy. The next morning she heard a loud knocking on her door. It was Arul. 'Come quickly, Amy. You must see what I've discovered!' He led Amy to the dormitories where the young girls were still sleeping. He pointed to the ground. 'See those large paw-prints where the earth is soft – that is the tiger's feet marks.'

Amy turned pale at the thought. 'Our dear children were in danger, but Jesus was guarding them.' Arul and Amy followed the tiger's tracks. He had even walked past the cows tied up close to the kitchen. 'I'm so glad you're here, Arul. We must build a wall around the building to stop wild beasts that wander down from the hills.'

As soon as men started work on it, a local man claimed that the land was his and they should stop. His lawyer even said the new nursery had to be pulled down. This man had never said this while Mr Walker was alive or in the thirteen years Amy had been living in Dohnavur. Everyone took this problem to the Lord in prayer. Amy never heard from the local man or his lawyer again.

Money to fight a court case would have been hard to spare from all the building needs. One man, willing to give a great deal of money to Amy, insisted on its being used for evangelistic work, not for buildings. 'Oh, Ponnammal,' sighed Amy, 'doesn't he know souls are fastened into bodies? You can't get the souls out and separate them. You can't pitchfork souls into heaven.'

'But have you heard from the Government lately?' Ponnammal asked. 'They said that they would give us teachers.'

Amy's frown deepened. 'Now we have teachers of our own I hope we will not need to accept the Government's offer,' she told Ponnammal.' Accepting the Government's grant, however generous, would mean joining the state exam system and bringing in books I don't want our children reading. God has provided for our needs in amazing ways and he will continue to do this. We must have faith and remember that he hears and answers our prayers.'

Prayer for more nursery building went on being answered. A woman in England wanted to give money in memory of her mother who had just died. The gift was £200, an enormous sum, but much needed. Amy loved Hudson Taylor's saying, 'God's work, done in God's way, will never lack God's supplies.'

Another blow caused Amy grief the year after Thomas died. In July 1913, she received a cable telling her that her mother had died. Her last letter to Amy a few days before had said, 'You are being carried along in God's almighty protecting arms of love and care.' With this comfort Amy carried on. She had always enjoyed writing poems and songs. Now she poured out her feelings in verse. She wrote some poetry while sitting up all night with sick children. If she was travelling in the hot, jolting bandy cart she had to remember the verses to write down later. Two songs were written on the brown paper wrapped round a large bottle of medicine she was taking back to Dohnavur.

And whilst she was in the middle of doing all that writing Amy was completely surprised to receive a letter from Queen Mary, offering her sympathy and encouragement. The King, George V, and his wife were in India as Emperor and Empress of India. A lady who knew Amy had told the Queen about Amy's work at Dohnavur. Amy had even been asked by the Government to supply details of the selling of girls to work in temples. Laws were finally passed to protect children from these practices.

However, Amy remarked that 'India knows how to evade laws. As these are laws made by a foreign, ruling power, they will often be ignored. But we must keep on working for these children - the little ones that we have rescued and the ones still in danger.'

This is what Amy did and the children loved her. One evening she was looking after five babies on her own. All of them were ready for their next feed. Unfortunately, the cows in the village had been brought in late for milking. When this happened Amy knew she just had to wait for the milk delivery. As the babies could not have all this explained to them, they simply cried. As it became darker they cried more loudly. The boy whose job it was to light their lamps did not show up, either, so the howling and whimpering got worse.

Ponnammal, always alert for problems Amy might have, brought a lamp to her. Amy let the light fall on their toys, a china doll's head broken away from its body and several small rattles. None of this made the babies feel better. One grabbed the doll's head and threw it on the floor. Still the milk did not arrive. Amy moved the lamp so that its light fell upon her. Seeing this, all five babies crawled towards her and were soon contentedly enjoying their cuddles.

With the outbreak of World War I well-meaning people began to offer unasked-for advice to Amy. 'What are you going to do with all those children in the future?' was a typical comment. Amy had already faced up to those kinds of fears in a poem which expressed her faith 'Hath he ever failed you yet? Never, never, so why fret?'

People back home in England saw the poems and letters from Amy, and a missionary society asked her to write about Dohnavur for their magazine. Amy sent them the story of her work, making clear the difficulty of rescuing temple girls. She wrote about the successful rescues, the problems with buildings and the babies who died from dysentery. The society returned what she had written, saying they needed stories with happy endings for their readers.

Amy had more success with her biography of Thomas Walker. She wanted the hidden life of service he gave to India to be more widely known. The typewriter someone had sent her was put to very good use. Soon stories of the children, their rescue, their funny sayings and their growing understanding of the gospel stories, were delighting readers back in England. Walker's biography was her ninth book.

A story told by a little girl called Leela was one Amy told in her fifth book:

The bad devil, Satan, was once good and lived in heaven. One day all the angels came to sing to God. Then Satan was angry at this. He was very rude to God. That bad, bad devil said, 'I want to sit in God's chair and make God sing to me!' So God took him and tumbled him down out of heaven.

Hundreds of Children

Amy knew that, to many people, the devil Leela told her story about was only imaginary or a subject for jokes. However, in India she saw him behind the idols of the heathen, wanting people to worship anything except the true God of Love. When she had first tried to find out about the temple girls, Satan had blinded the Government, and even other missionaries, to what was really going on. Amy was working for Satan's enemy, so expected to have opposition. Just like soldiers in the Great War raging far away, Amy knew frequent attacks and defeats. Deaths among the babies and her fellow-workers were heart-breaking for their Amma.

She often talked this over with Ponnammal and together they would pray about it. 'Now you have lost your strong support in Mr Walker, God will comfort you. He knows you have no other arm to rely on so he will be all your help.'

'We rest our hearts upon God, leaving what we do not know or understand to his love. That love has led me always in my life. The peace of God stays with me,' Amy told her.

And God's peace would also be with Ponnammal. For several months Ponnammal had been in pain but she concealed this and carried on helping Amy. But once Amy was told of Ponnammal's pain, she took her to a Salvation Army hospital south of Dohnavur, much nearer than the one at Bangalore. The doctor there diagnosed cancer and operated immediately. Amy stayed with her as the staff left in charge at Dohnavur were now more than capable of running things on their own, at least for a little while. Three months later Ponnammal was declared fit to go home and the two friends joyfully set out for Dohnavur. However, within a few weeks Ponnammal was again helpless with pain so a third operation was carried out. This time it was a success.

To outsiders it seemed that Amy went from one crisis to another. The war brought problems. Money dwindled in its value. Post was lost by enemy action, and it took months for donors to realise their cheques had never reached Amy. Yet Amy never refused to take in any temple child brought to her. Just before the war she had bought a large field to make into a market garden. Mission staff at Dohnavur received training in growing vegetables, and enough money came in to pay for this and the first planting. £50 came from a woman whose brother had been killed in action. He had left her the money in his will.

In 1915 Ponnammal's cancer returned. She suffered terrible pain so had to take strong pain-killers. She longed to be able to go on helping Amy, 'I had hoped to be able to stay with you and help you to bear the burden but it is not to be.'

Amy made the funeral a celebration because she knew that this was what Ponnammal would have wished. She had after all met her Saviour face to face. Ponnammal's bedroom was filled with brightly coloured flowers. White, scented flowers were laid round her body. Villagers and children followed her to the grave, many little ones dressed in blue, or white and yellow.

Ponnammal's father had been staying with them in her illness and was moved by the funeral, 'In all my seventy years I have never seen anything like this. I'm glad my granddaughter is staying here with you.'

But how empty and dreary the compound seemed to Amy with no Ponnammal there. She had been a loyal, unselfish friend and was irreplaceable.

To take her mind off her loss, Amy decided to take a group of girls for a holiday in the cool of the hills when the September heat returned. While the girls enjoyed a happy time together, Amy herself was very ill. She wrote in her journal, 'I have prayed, "Do not let me be ill and a burden or anxiety to anyone. Let me not die of a lingering illness. Oh, Lord, forgive this prayer if it is wrong."'

She returned to Dohnavur only to discover that Arulai, another mission worker, was ill. She had kidney disease so no medical treatment could save her. Again Amy spent hours in prayer for her. To everyone's relief Arulai gradually felt better and, by the following year, was completely recovered. Such healing was seen as a miracle which encouraged and gave joy to everyone who knew her.

And with Arulai recovered Amy again thought of taking the girls away on a holiday. Amy had been invited to take some of the older girls to Madras on an educational, sight-seeing trip. So she decided to do just that.

The busy port was fascinating to the children. They visited the harbour and the beaches. For the first time they saw a railway-station, motor-cars, telegraph wires and a palace. They even went to a cinema.

Here the girls were alarmed at first, thinking the pictures were alive. When war news was shown they were astonished at the speed of the soldiers' walk. Though this was actually just the result of early film camera work, Amy took the chance to urge them to follow their lively example. She had often teased others about the slow Indian walk.

But the girls needed no persuading to run fast when they saw the bright blue waters of the Indian Ocean. They ran straight in, laughing and giggling, until the water was right up to their knees.

On her return from Madras a letter was waiting for Amy. It was quite an important one. The Church Missionary Society had asked Amy to speak at a meeting. She was reluctant, partly because she never liked to draw attention to herself. She felt, too, that it could harm the children by revealing where they lived when rescued. Wearing a sari, as she always did, would be frowned upon by many of the British at the meeting. One of the ways they had poked fun at her for years was to dismiss her like Joseph's brothers had, as 'a dreamer of dreams.'

Amy, therefore, began her talk with 'I had a dream last night. I thought I had come to this meeting and an elderly missionary was asked to pray. 'Oh Lord', he said, 'here we are, met together for yet another meeting. You know how tired we are of meetings. Help us to get through this one.'

They all laughed at this and her audience were soon listening intently to a lively account of the work God had given her.

And Amy found that meetings like this could be quite good in spreading the word about the needs of the mission. As the numbers of children at Dohnavur grew to be in the hundreds, Amy had to spend more time in finding the right workers. She did not want anyone to come out with a romantic or sentimental idea of the life there. She wanted them to enjoy the flowers, babies and bright faces but, 'under the sweetness there is a real cross,' she would admit. 'It is hard to tell unsuitable candidates that they cannot join us. It is even harder to tell someone who has already been here that he or she cannot stay. I must, therefore, give a clear picture of life in India, be it at a meeting or in a letter or conversation.'

She wrote to one person, 'Bring to India a strong sense of humour and no sense of smell'.

She also made clear the high standard expected. 'Prayer is the core of our day. Without it, the day would collapse. But how can you pray with one you have a grudge against or someone you have been criticising to someone else?'

Amy wanted only people who, in their own way of life, could show the Lord Jesus to the idol-worshippers around them. They needed to be loyal to the family they came to join. The love within that family was, in Amy's view, only possible if the missionaries themselves were close to the God of love.

She wrote to an accepted candidate: 'My prayer for you is that you should be ready for anything, any suffering, any misunderstanding, any blame, anything for Jesus' sake.'

When new missionaries arrived they found, like Amy, that the Tamil language could be depressingly difficult. If you wanted to learn the basics of the language it could take you two years.

'Shall I ever be able to have any time to help you, or will it always be Tamil study? It is dreadful sometimes to think how feebly I press on,' was a typical complaint.

To help them Amy either rented a village house for the pupil or sent them to stay with a friendly Hindu family. Though tough at first, this was a really practical way of learning everyday Tamil.

But Amy was good at remembering how she had felt when she first came to Bangalore. 'One thing I really enjoyed there was my own bathroom.' So Amy decided to give every missionary a small room with a large water jar, a basin and dipper. A dip in the floor with a drain meant the 'bather' could pour water over herself.

As the lady of courage who had founded Dohnavur and an author of many books, she did not know that her reputation over-awed new recruits. However, after only a few weeks of working with her they soon felt part of a team and looked up to her with love as their leader.

They soon found out that her advice never to eat anything they had seen a fly on, was to be ignored for she did not follow it herself. She was a gifted actress. They could be taken in the first time they saw her bent over a stick, head covered and mimicking a conversation she heard between a villager and one of the children. When she pretended to be a Tamil bus conductor, everyone enjoyed the performance. She was simply very good company.

Buying the Grey Jungle

Amy's good company was certainly one of the ingredients which meant that everyone enjoyed holidays on the forest-covered slopes above Dohnavur. The foothills rose to over three thousand feet in places, with a beautiful mountain range towering above. Fresh cool air was a welcome change from the suffocating heat of the plains. Amy rented a bungalow from the Forest Department and took groups of children to stay there. Below the house a mountain river rushed along, then tumbled in a waterfall down to a deep, quiet pool. The children loved to scramble over the rocks to find mosses, ferns and flowers to take back to the house. As it had been empty for a year and had a cement floor, it could be damp and cold at times. Water had to be heated, cooking-stoves brought and set up, and latrines had to be dug. Everything else they needed had to be carried up there.

Amy's enthusiasm for the outdoor life was matched by that of the children. They loved to find elephant tracks, bears' dens, deer and tiger spoor and even the local monster spider. They watched, fascinated, as it spun its huge web from one tree trunk to another. Every time Amy took a new group of girls to stay there she would teach them to swim in the pool. 'Anyone who can't swim will not be able to come here again. You can have a lovely time in the pool and the rivers once you can swim. You will be safe and enjoy yourself.' Teaching them, though, could be dangerous. One day a girl dragged Amy under and they both nearly drowned. 'That wasn't too bad now, was it?' said Amy to her cheerfully, 'not bad enough to tell the others about when we get back to Dohnavur.'

Even here Amy's sense of humour led her to playing a trick. With three other girls, she was coming back from a walk when she spotted the others walking up to the house. She took the girls with her to hide behind the trees and started making growling noises. The others rushed in alarm up to the house and came out carrying large sticks. Thinking Amy's group was in danger, they bravely went down the hill making as much noise as they could to scare the bears away. Amy then emerged from the trees. 'Whatever is the matter? What are you doing?'

'We heard the bears and thought they would eat you.' A little girl behind Amy giggled and gave the game away.

Amy soon realised that the bungalow was too small for the numbers who needed to stay there. As always, prayer and discussion took place first. Amy and two other missionaries began looking for a good site to build on. They climbed up one day to a very steep place, a ravine with a high mountain backing it. In front lay an open grassy plain with a view across to the seacoast. All three thought it would be just the right spot for their very own holiday home.

The Muslim owner was willing to sell to them, but they would have to buy all thirty-seven acres of hillside. This would include a river, waterfall, tall trees and pool. All that was needed was the money. Next morning when the mail was opened at Dohnavur, Amy had a letter from a lawyer in Ireland, telling her that a friend who had just died had left her one hundred pounds. This they all took as a sign that God wanted them to go ahead, so they bought the Muslim's land which he called 'The Grey Jungle'.

That was the start of their troubles. The carpenter turned out to be unreliable, the stone-masons could not be trusted and heavy rains held up the work. There were disagreements amongst the workmen over which caste-members could do certain parts of the building. Some stone embedded in mud was used for the walls. One day, before the roof was on, there was a sudden heavy downpour. All the masons ran to take shelter in their huts. As they had left the walls uncovered they could have fallen down as the mud dissolved in the rain. Amy had to come to the rescue herself. With mission workers and some of the oldest children she passed up mats to cover the roofless building.

With patience and determination, Amy finally steered the workers towards completion of the building, which she named 'The Forest House.' Once they had finished, Amy set out to explore the whole area. The Indian servants followed wherever she led them, up steep cliffs and past waterfalls. 'It has all been worth it,' she exclaimed one evening, 'it is God's house and he has overseen its building'.

'The devil put all those problems in our way, I'm sure,' a colleague replied. 'Well, he's lost two of his followers through it. Do you remember those two Hindu carpenters who came to our gospel meetings? They came to see me today and have asked to be baptised. They would like to have the service in the pool below the Forest House.'

All the children loved 'their' house. They swept the paths, decorated it with flowers and respected all animal life as Amy had taught them to do. The exception was that if a scorpion or one of the local poisonous snakes was found inside the house, they would have to be killed. They were too far from medical help to take chances. By the end of the war, in 1918, there were plans underway to build more houses in the Grey Jungle. Amy showed her gratitude to the many who gave towards the building in the vivid letters she sent to them.

'Green forest stretches as far as the eye can see, rising to the mountains, leaving bare only the rocky tops. In front of our red-roofed house, the trees drop sharply down to our pool. It is jade-green, deep enough for diving. Its floor is all clean white sand. We sometimes see a blue kingfisher. The holiday children and our helpers turn into water-babies. If you have troubles, the pool washes them off.'

Picnics with Amy were special events. A servant would go ahead of the party, cutting a path through the brushwood with a large knife. The girls and the servants would carry the tea-things, climbing carefully to avoid breaking the china crockery. While they were all seated around her, Amy would say, or sing, her latest poem about life in the forest.

The elephant comes with a tramp, tramp, tramp.
The elephant comes with a stamp, stamp, stamp.
Through forest and over marshy ground
His great big fat feet pound and pound
With a rumpety-dumpety-crumpety sound.

These were holidays, though, and most of Amy's time was still spent in fighting for the temple girls. As the girls were bought and sold for a good profit they were not given up easily by family or by temple women. A girl called Kohila, which meant Cuckoo, had been happily settled at Dohnavur. Just after Kohila's fifth birthday Amy had a letter from her guardians, demanding Kohila's return. If they did not get her back, they threatened to charge Amy with the crime of kidnapping. She could be sentenced to seven years in prison for this. For Amy the only solution was to put Kohila where she would never be found. She arranged sanctuary for her with friends hundreds of miles away.

She could not go herself, as an English woman travelling with an Indian girl would have aroused suspicion. So Arul Dasan, the one who had warned Amy about the tiger prints, offered to take the little girl to safety. Six days later he came back. Kohila was safe. However, Arul's tired, lined face showed how dangerous his journey had been. 'I took a houseboat through Tinnevelly, as we planned. I thought I'd been found out because two men kept staring at me and whispering. I heard them say something about Kohila's court case in Madras and thought I was going to lose her. They left the boat at its next stop and I didn't see them again. Is there any more news from the lawyers?' he asked.

'No,' replied Amy, 'but I have had such joy and comfort from everyone that I do not fear imprisonment. Do you know, several colleagues have actually offered to serve the sentence for me? I've explained that the British judge won't allow that.'

Amy did not like breaking the law as kidnapping in other circumstances was awful. But she could not return her temple girls to the misery and cruelty they had been rescued from, so could only refuse the court's order. Soon, though, she heard that the court case against her had been dismissed and Kohila was allowed to come home to Dohnavur again. They met her at a large railway station crowded with Indian travellers. Suddenly Amy heard a shout and Kohila was leaping up at her with hugs and kisses.

There were now over five hundred children living at Dohnavur. Many had been abandoned when only babies and sold to the temple women, so their parents could not be traced. Soon unwanted babies were being handed over, merely because they were very ill, or deaf, or unable to walk properly. Once again, Amy's longing for a hospital led to more prayers. These children needed specialist help, particularly the deaf ones.

Thousands of miles away in the Scottish capital, Edinburgh, a young woman called Jean was teaching Sunday School. She had wanted to help the deaf children who sat in church so cut-off and silent. She decided to train to teach the deaf and did this after University. Her parents had a great interest in Amy's work, so when Jean heard about the needs in Dohnavur she was soon on her way there.

Then, a few years after the war, Amy was helped by an Indian church to buy land near the southern coast. Her plan was to build a school and home for disabled children, sick girls and workers in need of a rest. There was some opposition from local priests, but that didn't come to anything. As the land was high up above the sea, cool, health-giving breezes blew round the buildings. Children with learning difficulties, the delicate and the deaf loved their trips to the seaside here.

As soon as she could, Amy got to know the priests and the local Hindus. Some who lived in a nearby village were even afraid a disease would ruin their crops if Christians were looking down on them all the year round. As the old head priest got to know Amy he confided in her, 'I've no joy, no peace, no hope. I've served my god faithfully, all for nothing.' Amy could speak of the God of love to him but, like so many, he listened without finding out any more. Men like this reminded Amy of the little boys she had seen on the juggernaut. 'If no one helps them they too will end up like this priest with no joy, no hope and no knowledge of the one true God.'

Fear at the Theatre Schools

The memory of the Juggernaut procession never really left Amy's mind. The devotion the people had given to a lump of stone shaped like a seated man saddened her. At Dohnavur she aimed to bring her girls up in a loving atmosphere and to believe in a kind, loving God. Her worst memory of that day was the young boys. They had been taken from their homes, probably sold by their parents, and placed with temple women to be trained, as the girls were. Like them, the boys would be punished cruelly if they tried to go home.

An Indian friend told Amy about another horrific trade. Little boys were sold to theatre companies. Amy could not bear to see children suffering. Her friend warned her that the so-called theatre schools were upsetting, but Amy would not back out and agreed to go with him. To remain unnoticed Amy again stained her face and arms brown with coffee.

They arrived outside a building with barred windows and a heavy, strong door. Amy's friend knocked and it opened just enough to reveal the lined face of a very old woman. 'Are the children well?' asked Amy's friend.

'There are no children here,' was the reply.

'The boys,' he persisted, 'the boys who learn here.'

'No boys learn here,' she snarled and slammed the door.

'I'll take you to a travelling theatre,' Amy's friend said, 'we might get a clue there.'

It was now late at night and the narrow streets were crowded. They found the theatre and bought tickets. Amy casually asked the ticket-seller, 'Where do the children live?' Thinking they were ordinary Indian play-goers he gave them directions. These led them through a maze of streets to a very run-down part of town. The door of the house was open, perhaps because it was not long to the performance. A man stood outside.

Amy spoke first, 'We have come to see the children.'

He showed them in through a large courtyard. A tiny boy ran up to her. 'Come and meet my friends.'

He took her to a large, high-walled room where about two dozen boys were learning their parts aloud. How thankful Amy felt to have this opportunity to talk to the boys. They chatted to her about their training and life in the house. Her easy, gentle manner soon won them over.

'If I'd worn a European woman's dress and hat I would never have got this far. Or if I'd had blue eyes,' she thought to herself.

Suddenly, an angry man burst in, shouting, 'Off to your lessons, boys.'

One six-year-old boy who had sat on Amy's lap while she chatted away in Tamil, walked away slowly.

Was he new, recently taken away from his mother? Amy bent over and put her hands together in the Indian way and the man in charge did the same, thinking she was Indian. They returned to the theatre and took their seats.

The curtains opened to reveal the boy who had led them to the rehearsal room. He was wearing shiny clothes and imitation jewels and was sitting on a throne. He played an Indian flute expertly and acted well all through the play. The audience clapped him enthusiastically and roared their approval. The boy who had sat on Amy's lap appeared, looking very anxious and troubled. She could soon see why. At the side of the stage stood the rehearsal master, holding a long cane. Although some of the actors were as old as sixteen, it was clear that for the audience it was the charm of the younger boys on stage that brought them to the theatre.

'How I long to storm into that house and take these little boys away. All children deserve the chance of a normal life, education and family love. But I know that the Government and local rulers are covering all this up. When I demand changes they tell me that I am exaggerating.' Amy turned her back on the theatre very reluctantly, wondering what would happen to the little six year old boy who had sat on her lap so nicely.

Back at Dohnavur, her friends wisely pointed out that she did not have the strength to take on any more work. Besides, boys and girls could not live in the same compound in India. She should leave God to bring out someone else to carry out such new work. Amy still longed to help the young boys but she made up her mind to go on praying. God would find a way to help them.

One night Amy and the nurse, Mabel, heard a bullock-cart coming up to the verandah. This was very late for anyone to be calling on them so they hurried outside. A weary-looking helper got down from the cart and put a baby into Amy's arms. 'He's a little boy. I know we have only girls but the most dreadful temple woman was going to buy him. I couldn't let that happen.'

'We will take him in. Of course we will,' said Amy, 'and we will pray for more boys.'

There was plenty of room for another nursery in the compound, but extra money was needed to pay for buildings. Prayers were answered and, each day as the post was opened, gifts of money arrived. Baby boys did, too. Other missionaries trusted and respected Amy for the work they had seen her do to help girls. Now they helped her find boys in danger of being sold to the temples and theatres.

But as the boys and girls kept arriving and as the post-war value of money went down, Amy faced some hard financial decisions. They always bought food in bulk as that saved expense, but one day Amy needed coins to pay for grain, not cheques. As she had no cash it seemed that, apart from milk from their own cows, little food could be provided. A letter from a friend in another part of India came in that morning's post, a rather plump letter. 'I wanted to lie down in the heat of midday but something made me get on with your letter instead. I've had these forty pounds put aside in rupees ready to send you. Today I felt I should go and do it at once.' This was yet another proof to Amy that she was where God wanted her to be.

Amy's life seemed to be full of big and little examples of God's provision. She was always delighted to entertain visitors, whether people visiting India or working in other parts of the country. There was a special guest room kept at Dohnavur and the visitor would share meals with Amy and her helpers, staying for free. One January, a minister Amy had known in the Lake District arrived. They had decided to put a card in the guest-room, saying what the day's food cost, as their resources were low. But Amy could not bear to think that his welcome would be this card. She took it away, filled his room with roses from their gardens, and told him nothing about their money problems. On the second day of his visit he stood with Amy, watching the children going to and fro in huge numbers. He suddenly spoke, 'His compassions fail not, and that means this.' He put his hand into his pocket and drew out a bundle of notes which he gave to Amy. 'I have put in extra to make up for the war's effect on your money. Everything in the work I have seen here has the touch of God so naturally upon it.'

And one of the examples of God's love and work in Dohnavur was the love and work of Amy herself. When a dreadful cholera outbreak swept through the local village, Amy would not take the missionaries, helpers and servants away from their work with the children, so set out to help by herself. She carried a bucket of medicines, tins, rags, bottles and disinfectants. Constant sickness weakened the patients. Amy worked tirelessly, day after day, but many deaths could not be prevented. She asked the local Christian leader, an Indian, to carry her heavy bucket, but he said he preferred to preach or pray for the ill. Even the village chief simply watched as she cleaned out the huts with disinfectant.

Amy's example of love and compassion sometimes encouraged others to live a similar life, but often people's selfish natures just got in the way. Sometimes missionaries and ministers in other parts of India asked if members of their churches could adopt a child from Dohnavur. After thorough checks they sent parents to Amy to take away a child they wanted. This worked out very well for a few but for most it was a disaster. It turned out that all some parents wanted was a cheap servant. Amy had to rescue many for the second time in their lives. One child had cuts on her face and burns on her arms and legs. These badly-treated children were overjoyed to be back in the safety and love that Dohnavur gave them.

More reliable Indian men came to help care for the boys. They also worked to rescue any they heard were in danger. Arul Dasan told Amy he had heard that a woman in his village was planning to sell her four-year-old son to a theatre trainer. He was a handsome, intelligent little boy and she would be paid well for him. When Arul next went to visit the home he discovered that the woman had left, taking her son with her. But he would not give up the chase. He tracked the woman to a town a hundred miles away and went there to speak to her. He pleaded with her not to sell her son into a life of misery. It began to look as though he was making progress. She was afraid that it might be wrong to sell her son if this man was telling her his God had sent him to fetch the boy. At last she agreed to let the boy be taken to Dohnavur. Arul quickly took the child and left at once for the bazaar. There he paid a goldsmith to file through the gold chains the boy wore on his wrists and ankles. Without these, the journey back to Dohnavur would be a safer one.

'Stop doing that!' a voice cried. It was his mother. 'Give him back to me. My sister has just called. When I told her about you she cursed me in the name of our gods. They will punish me. I must get my son back. He will be happy in the theatre. He won't miss me. A few beatings will be good for him.' She seized the boy and hurried away. Arul had to return to Dohnavur without him.

He went on helping Amy and, a few weeks later, did recover another child safely. Arul decided to have one more try for the four-year-old. He found his mother again and asked her about the boy. 'He's yours for the taking. He's no good to me. I won't get any money for him now,' she grumbled.

'So where is he, then?' he asked.

'That's him over there, in the corner.'

Arul saw she was pointing to a bundle of rags and went over to look. He realised it was the boy, but his face was covered in smallpox and he was blind. The theatre would not want him now.

'My sister stopped me giving him to you. I could have made good money before he fell ill.'

Arul knew that Dohnavur was the one place where handicaps made no difference to the treatment he would have. Amy made sure all the children were loved and cared for.

And it was this policy of love and care that was at the centre of Amy's work with children. In 1927 Amy decided to become independent of the Church Missionary Society and call the mission officially 'The Dohnavur Fellowship.' The CMS generously gave her the bungalow and land she lived on. Amy wrote a statement of the Fellowship's aims:

To save children in moral danger

To train them to serve others

To care for the desolate and the suffering

To make known the love of our Heavenly Father, especially to the people of India.

Despite requests from other missionaries, Amy would not have any special mention of herself as leader, so the statement says that 'the human leader seeks, with other members of the Council, to carry out the will of the unseen leader, the Lord Jesus Christ.'

This shunning of the limelight did not surprise her friends as they knew the story of the medal. In 1919 Amy had received a telegram from the Governor of Madras. He congratulated her on being awarded the Kaiser-i-Hind Medal for her services to the people of India. She was so shocked by this that she wanted to refuse it. 'It troubles me to have something so different from our Lord Jesus who was despised and rejected, not kindly honoured,' was her reply.

At last she was persuaded to accept the honour, but she resolutely refused to attend a presentation ceremony in Madras. With this, the Governor of Madras had to be satisfied. There was no shifting Amy once she had made her mind up.

Celebrations

'Where did I come from, Amma?' a little girl called Moonflower asked Amy one day.

'You are my daughter,' Amy replied. 'You are here because, first, God brought you and then, because we loved you very much.'

With many of the children rescued as babies there was no way of finding out when they had been born. Amy herself had loved birthdays at home in Ireland with all her brothers and sisters. She did not want her Indian family to miss out on all that fun. 'We record the date the baby arrives here at Dohnavur and call that the child's Coming Day. We make that special, just like a birthday. What a popular idea that's turned out to be. Moonflower will love hers.'

'Of course she will,' agreed one of the other workers. 'She is already too excited to sleep. And the other girls are gathering flowers to decorate Moonflower's room for her.'

Very early the next day Moonflower awoke and had to wait impatiently for her visit to Amma. 'Happy Coming Day', Amy greeted her. 'Here's your card and your special present.'

'Mm, this soap smells just like those large white flowers in the nursery garden', said Moonflower. She waited then, but could not help glancing over to the large blue cupboard in the corner of Amy's room.

'All right, then. Let's open the doors and see what you want to choose.'

Moonflower followed Amy across the room and gazed at the colourful assortment of gifts on the shelves. This part of the birthday always took quite a long time.

For special birthdays there would be a feast. The table would be covered with sweet things that were too expensive for everyday meals. Moonflower loved the payasam, made with rice and palm-sugar, honey cakes, halva with sultanas and almonds, and fried cashews. Slices of fresh mangoes and pineapples slipped down very well after all this.

However one year food was short and money down, too, so Amy warned the girls about this. 'For birthday celebrations this month I can give you oranges and pineapples from our Forest House. The only biscuits left are the hard, twisty ones. I'm sorry, we have to be careful with food at the moment. We just can't afford to buy anything more.'

'That doesn't matter,' one little girl told her, 'As long as we can all sit together, it'll be fine. We'll all put on head-dresses of flowers and enjoy it just like a feast'.

It was a thrill for Amy when the children could say things like that. She wanted them to be loving and unselfish. Every Monday morning at meetings in the compound, everyone repeated together the thirteenth chapter of the first letter Paul wrote to the Christians in the Greek town of Corinth. This was recited in Tamil and in English. They only had to look at Amy to see Paul's words put into action, 'Love suffers long and is kind'.

Amy remembered the long prayer meetings she had sat through as a very small girl. At Dohnavur she did not make the children sit still with nothing to do. She gave the youngest brightly-coloured flags. During some of the songs they could stand up and wave these. Older ones would have tambourines, maracas and bells to play on during the singing. Occasionally when some of the children first arrived at Dohnavur they missed the Hindu festivals with processions, flowers, music and dancing. However as they got older Amy made sure to tell them about the cruel imprisonment that they had been rescued from. And many, many, children had been rescued from that torture. It was something that Amy was always thankful for.

And with so many children in the mission it was a wonder that more quarrels didn't happen, but quarrels happen in all families. When two little girls fell out with each other, Amy sometimes tied their pigtails together so that they had to walk together for the rest of the day. It was surprising how quickly this sorted out the trouble between them. One girl made a lot of trouble for the others by lying. As nothing Amy did stopped her, she finally sent the girl to fetch the strap. She sat her on her lap and began telling her how the Lord Jesus took on himself the punishment for human sins. Amy then beat her own arm with the strap, instead of the little girl's.

One girl thought she had found a clever way of avoiding being punished for her bad behaviour. A teacher sent her to see Amy with a note about what had happened. The girl stood in front of her with a bright smile.

'Where is the note?' asked Amy.

At this the girl smiled widely and declared with a chuckle, 'I swallowed it!'

Another little girl with a rather mischievous smile could never keep a secret. For her Amy thought up a little test.

'I'm planning a trip to Madras for you and your friends soon. It's a secret for now, so promise me not to tell them yet.'

The little girl promised, eagerly, not to say a word. Half-an-hour later the girls were excitedly asking Amy all about the holiday. Amy turned to face the culprit.

'I keep my promise, Amma, really I did. I keep it very hard,' she blurted out. 'I said to them, "We are not going to London, we are not going to Calcutta, we are not going to Bombay." Then they guess and say, "We are going to Madras," and I say nothing at all to them.'

One girl, when asked if she had been caned in school that day, told Amy, 'No, not exactly caned, I was sitting beside a very naughty girl and the teacher meant to cane her, but the cane fell on me by mistake.'

The presence of so many energetic and mischievous children at Dohnavur meant that the work was never dull. But it also meant that there was plenty of work to do.

Amy shared out the chores in her Dohnavur family. Being in India those jobs were different from the ones in Ireland. Children twisted rice, picked tamarind fruit, peeled palm-shoots, watered the flowers and dusted their rooms. Older girls had their own vegetable and fruit gardens. They could sell the produce to the housekeeper at the going rate and then save up this money in clay pots. Once a year these were broken and everyone running the garden had a say in how the money should be spent.

Although all the children were Indian and Amy had none of her own, she often saw them getting up to mischief like her own childhood pranks. One night the girls heard a band playing near the compound. They guessed this meant a wedding in the village. As celebrations really got underway very late at night, one of the older girls woke the others up at midnight. They climbed onto the garden wall to have a good view of the marriage procession, the dancing and fireworks. When the Indian workers found their room empty, they felt frightened. A search-party soon found the girls who then had to go back to bed.

Early next morning they went to see Amy.

'I'm sorry we upset everyone,' one girl said quietly. 'We didn't think about what would happen if they found us gone and thought that we had been snatched away.'

'I'm glad you see what a scare you gave everyone,' Amy acknowledged. 'But I can see that now you're older you will enjoy weddings. Next time I hear there's going to be one I will take you all to see it,' Amy smiled.

The children also enjoyed Amy's songs and verses. One they loved to chant loudly together on Forest picnics was:

> Take good advice and promptly go,
> Abominable Mosquito.

On her birthday they loved to sing her own song to her:

> Lord of the brooding blue
> Of pleasant summer skies,
> Lord of each little bird that through
> The clear air flies,
> 'Tis wonderful to me
> That I am loved by Thee.

One Easter-time she told a story to make real to the children the selfless, loving work the Lord Jesus did at Calvary.

'I have two baby mynah birds, Huz and Buz. They have no feathers yet so are like two sooty balls of fur.

They have immense mouths which they keep wide open nearly all the time. They are yelling "Give! Give! Give!" even after being fed. Some people are like that with Jesus. "Give me happiness. Give me an easy time. Give me all I want." Do you want to be like Huz and Buz? Think of how much you can give Jesus and of all he has done for us.'

Arul was as interested in all of nature as Amy was. As he grew up at Dohnavur he caught her enthusiasm. He loved to use the microscope and she would explain how the chlorophyll in the cells he could see enlarged and made the leaves green. He collected plants and birds' feathers, and his study turned him into a mine of information for the younger ones to turn to. Amy's prayers for more men missionaries were answered and the boys could go out on trips together. One of their favourite haunts was the lake that appeared in the monsoons, only a little way from Dohnavur. Here they could go canoeing.

And then the car arrived - which intrigued both the boys and the girls. In the New Year of 1923 a generous donor gave a Ford car to Dohnavur. This saved Amy both time and strength. About the same time a group of Indian Christians in a village at the foot of the mountains sent to Amy for help. The landlord was making life very difficult for them. One of the new male missionaries drove over there with Arul. They preached at the church on the Sunday, then reported back that support was needed. They bought a small house, set up a pharmacy and nurses went over to help the villagers. Before long the landlord was threatening to burn down their house and the church. For Hindus to stand out as Christians was always dangerous.

The landlord finally took them to court, claiming he owned the whole village. By paying a large bribe he made sure the court case went in his favour. All the Christian villagers moved to a field at the other side of the mission-house and rebuilt their houses.

Amy always believed that, with so much angry opposition from outside, everyone in Dohnavur needed to live in love and peace with one another. To bring that about, her rule was 'never to speak about, always to speak to.' By keeping to this, gossip and back-biting could be stopped. Workers and children would discuss face to face any worries or complaints.

But Amy faced the anger of local Hindus many times. She was often also on the wrong side of her own British law in India and that upset her. She expected opposition from Hindus, but not from her own people. One case threatened to wreck all the children's lives at Dohnavur. As it concerned a child in danger, Amy would not turn back once she had become involved.

One March night a woman brought her twelve year old daughter to Amy. 'Please protect us!' she begged. 'Muttammal is my only child. Now my husband is dead, his family want to get their hands on the fortune he left to her. Her uncle wants to marry her to a relative of his to get at the money.' Amy agreed to look after

Muttammal, and the mother left. A few weeks later the mother and the relatives demanded to have the girl returned. Amy had to let Muttammal go.

The very next month news came that the uncle had kidnapped her. It was then that the mother brought in police and lawyers. Amy found an English lawyer who thought he had a solution. He persuaded the other lawyers to give temporary custody of Muttammal to Amy. He had to accept two conditions: she would not give up her Hindu religion and she would keep to her caste while with Amy.

Muttammal, however, had put her faith in Jesus, so found these conditions hard. She had to cook her own food in a kitchen all by herself. She could not be baptised as that would break the other condition. A close watch had to be kept on her, as someone might try to tie a marriage jewel on her, and this would at once make Muttammal the legal possession of the future husband.

A final court hearing was arranged to decide where she was to live. The clerk read through almost forty pages of argument and then came to the decision, 'The girl must be returned to her mother. All court costs are to be paid by Miss Carmichael.' With a heavy heart, Amy returned to Dohnavur to break the sad news. However, when Amy arrived Muttammal had disappeared and no one knew where she had gone.

Weeks of anxiety followed. At last, after six months, a letter arrived, telling the whole story. Knowing how likely it was that the court would decide against Amy, a woman visitor from England, who had been staying at Dohnavur during the court case, helped Muttammal to escape. She dressed her as a Muslim boy and took her by a back gate out of the compound. Muttammal was then taken in a bandy cart to a mission-house. From there she was taken by a roundabout route to Sri Lanka, Singapore, Hong Kong and finally to missionaries in China. She stayed there for six years and then someone offered to take her to America. But Muttammal wanted to return to Amy, and this is exactly what she did when she reached eighteen years of age.

Just 260 Rupees

Amy gazed at the old carpenter in delight and amazement. 'Please, Amma, build a temple for our God,' he repeated. He was the only Christian in his village and Amy thought he was very brave. It took a lot of courage for a Hindu to ask to be baptised as a Christian. Amy was just about to agree to the proposal when the carpenter added, 'I will give two months' pay to help with the building.'

'You have spoken about the very thing closest to my heart,' Amy replied. 'We can still go to the local church but a place for prayer and our own special meetings would be wonderful. Thank you for being so generous. I will tell our children and workers about a building. It will be the "House of Prayer."'

The children gave Amy a special surprise by getting together to raise the money by not wasting what they already had. They sent her a note:

1. We won't waste soap and put the soap to dissolve in the water and sun.
2. We won't let the white ants get our saris. We will try to keep our saris without tearing.
3. We won't give our food to the crows and dogs and we won't spill milk.

The list went on and on in this way. Their efforts did save money and other gifts soon came in the post. Eventually one of the mission workers came to tell Amy the good news, 'We just need 260 rupees to finish the work.'

When the mail arrived that day Amy had a letter from America posted seven weeks before. 'Something made me decide to send you this extra bit of money, just to finish something, I thought'. The cheque was for one hundred dollars which, on exchange, was worth 260 rupees. The House of Prayer could be built.

And it was. It was a beautiful building covered with flowering vines. It had a tower in which tubular bells were hung. Morning and evening a hymn was played on the bells. Inside the building was a smooth red tile floor with a beautifully patterned carpet at one end, given by missionaries in Persia. Everyone sat on the floor, in the Indian manner, though a few chairs were kept there for anyone sick or elderly.

But a House of Prayer was only the beginning. More and more Amy felt the need for a hospital at Dohnavur. Although the new car was very useful, it was hardly the right thing to carry patients in to the hospital miles away. A hospital would not only cost a great deal, but would need missionary doctors to run it. The first to arrive, Dr. May Powell, must have been surprised to see that she would be working in a building that had first been a hen-house. They then built on four mat houses and added an Indian house to complete this make-shift hospital.

One afternoon, as Amy and a visitor were taking a walk they heard excited chatter coming from further down the hill. Suddenly a group of girls in blue saris came in sight. What were they calling out? 'One hundred pounds, one hundred pounds for the new hospital!' As the weeks and months went on, this early gift was added to by many small and large donations. To buy land for a hospital implied a belief that doctors and nurses would be given, too.

Within a year two male missionaries visited Dohnavur and stayed there for a while. The first to come was the grandson of someone Amy had known when living in the D.O.M.'s house in the Lake District. His name was Godfrey and he was on his way to China to work with the Children's Special Service Mission. It was soon obvious that he and Amy had a similar idea of missionary work and the same devotion to the Lord Jesus. The second to visit her was Godfrey's brother, Murray, a doctor and also on his way to serve in China. He stayed a little longer to carry out some operations. He and Dr. Powell worked tirelessly to remove troublesome tonsils and adenoids as well as other minor operations. They even carried on working in the evenings by lamplight as there was no electricity at Dohnavur yet. All three doctors had Amy's high ideals of love and service to God. After dinner everyone would get together to discuss the work at Dohnavur. As there were now eighty boys living there, Amy longed for more men to work with them.

Godfrey and Murray seemed just right for the work. However, both felt that it was China that God had called them to. Amy, though, was left with the strong impression that she should pray for both to work with her. Could she be mistaken? With horror she realised that she was actually breaking one of the Ten Commandments by coveting her neighbour's menservants. How could she pray to take workers away from China?

But God was in control of all these details. Godfrey fell seriously ill in China and was advised by doctors to go to a better climate for a rest. He at once thought of Dohnavur and returned there. Meanwhile, civil war had broken out in China. Many missionaries working inland were told to move to the port of Shanghai. Murray was among them and, as there was no let-up in the fighting, he asked for six-months' leave. He went straight to Dohnavur where there was plenty of work to be getting on with.

The work there was made slightly more difficult because of all the different religions of the patients. It meant that special cooking arrangements had to be made. A patient's family cooked all meals for him or her. The ward had to be divided into many separate cubicles for this purpose. 'The fishy smell will come over the wall,' complained one woman, a strict Hindu vegetarian. Muslims liked to kill and cook food in their own way, too. Murray and Amy could not run an Indian hospital like an English one. Even they had to insist though that hens could not be kept under beds until needed for meals.

Events in China prevented Murray's return and one day Amy was overjoyed to have a note from him asking, 'May I stay here?' She was now sixty-one and had worked in India for the last twenty-three years. She could now hand over responsibility for the boys as well as other sections of the work to Godfrey, who was still with them at Dohnavur and Murray took on all surgery at the hospital. Arul had made some enquiries about land near the compound suitable for their new hospital. A few weeks later, a telegram came for Amy, offering a gift of £1,000 towards the building costs.

The new hospital could not be built all at once as the money did not come in all at once. A Scotsman heard about the hospital and wrote to Amy, promising to pay for new surgical instruments, no matter what the price. The list was carefully made out and sent to him. Time passed and nothing more was heard. Almost a year later the mystery was solved. He had been badly injured in a motor accident. As soon as he was recovering, he sent the cheque as he had promised. A cable arrived from another supporter offering a thousand pounds for a maternity ward. That very generous gift also helped bring electric power to the hospital.

And the new hospital brought more opportunities for Amy and the staff to share their faith in Jesus. One day a man badly mauled by a tiger was brought in. It took a long time to deal with his wounds, so he had the opportunity to watch how these Christians lived. He became a Christian and began telling people in his village about the peace and joy he had found. When he asked for the doctor to come and teach in the village, Murray was eager to accept his invitation. When he arrived, a large group of men and women were sitting in silence waiting to hear what he had to say. They would have listened all night if he could have stayed. The change in their neighbour had made them think about the darkness in their Hindu beliefs. He had destroyed a shrine he had built near his house and had turned it into a cow-barn. In this way the hospital was changing local people's lives for the better.

Even in small, simple ways the staff and children at Dohnavur showed patients and relatives the love of Christ. Being put off to sleep before an operation was a new frightening experience for many patients. One little boy asked, 'Please sing me to sleep', so Amy sent a group of children to sing outside the operating theatre. If any grown-ups asked for this they were 'sung to sleep,' too. Some of the youngest children went into the hospital wards in the evening to sing for patients. They often carried coloured lanterns which made a cheerful ending to the day for everyone.

When Murray spoke at the opening of the hospital he said its purpose was: 'to be a place where people may come, not to be preached at, dosed and dealt with as cases, but to feel at home, to watch those who wash their bandages and dress their wounds to show them what the Lord Jesus had done for them.' At Christmas a tree was decorated for the child patients and presents given to them all. A feast was prepared by the father of a boy who had been helped in the hospital and everyone of all castes and religions were welcomed and enjoyed the celebration.

However, at this time it was sad to see that Amy had lost almost all the sight of one eye and often suffered from dreadful headaches. But she was so thankful to have Murray and Godfrey to be leaders for the boys and May Powell for the girls. Whatever might happen to Amy herself in the future, her boys and girls would be well cared for.

The Robber Chieftain

One of those leaders, Godfrey, had not been in India long before he knew exactly what he was taking on in South India. 'I was coming home from a walk one evening just as the procession had gone inside the temple and I could see the torches and the crowds around their god, framed in the arched entrance gate. Above it rose the great temple tower and it seemed in that moment as if the devil reigned here. The shouting of the crowds was like the laughter of the prince of evil, as he saw our feeble efforts to dislodge him. But I knew that God would reign, for he had spoken of victory over the devil.'

Amy nodded as he told her this, for this had been how she felt when first confronting idol-worship in India. She had once faced up to forces of heathen evil directly. That was the time that she met a robber chieftain named Raj.

In the crowded bazaars everyone loved to talk over the latest exploits of Red Tiger, as he was also called. British newspapers all over South India were calling him Robin Hood. From his hideout in the forests he swooped down on highway travellers. If they were clearly wealthy he stole money and food from them. He then gave away the stolen goods to the poor and elderly. Raj never killed anyone despite being an excellent shot, so good that he could kill a bird in flight.

His story was a very common one in that part of India. An enemy had accused him falsely to the police. This man hated him so much that he spread lies about him and probably bribed the court officials generously to win his case. Raj left his wife and children and found a hideaway on the densely-forested slopes of the mountains. Amy began praying for this daring outlaw. She then asked her Indian servants to find out if she could meet him. Her one thought was, 'Could I see him, and tell him of the Saviour?'

The Indian servants' gossip about Amy's interest in Raj soon reached the ears of the man himself. Like many others, he too had heard about this English woman and was curious. He knew she was up in the Grey Jungle so waylaid her there one day. 'Is this the Amma of Dohnavur, this small, neat woman in a blue sari?' he thought.

Amy, too, was having a good look at him. 'Immensely strong, every inch an athlete. Flashing eyes with an angry fire in them under those bushy black eyebrows,' she thought. 'See, we have tea here, and bread,' she said, and both sat down together.

Incredible as such a meeting seemed, Amy seized her opportunity. She listened to his tale of injustices. 'My case is hopeless. My enemy has made sure of that. Now I've heard my wife has died suddenly. Will you look after my three children?'

Amy was happy to do this for him. She told him the story of Jesus, a totally innocent person put to death as a criminal. Amy explained how Jesus had spent his life doing good to others but was willing to give his life as payment for others' sins. Raj listened eagerly and she gave him a Bible.

After that she heard stories about him from time to time. Once he was caught and put in a local prison. Two days later he escaped and sent his guard back with the handcuffs, 'Take these iron bangles back to the police-station for to that place they belong.' However, the police were right behind him and yet again he was found and put in prison. Amy visited him several times. He asked to be baptised and she got permission from the prison governor to allow this.

Amy was banned from visiting him again but she was allowed to write. His little daughter wrote to him telling him about her happy life at Dohnavur. Amy went on praying for this new convert. At his trial Raj pleaded guilty as he saw no other way out. As he was thought to be a dangerous prisoner he had his feet bound with a special type of chain. A week later he escaped again. Amy wondered if he would go back to his outlaw way of life. As a Christian he had confessed in court to all he had done that was wrong. If he took to highway robbery again he would lose his life.

Three hundred armed men led by two Englishmen scoured the countryside for Raj, without success. The police were starting to look incompetent and feared they would lose their jobs. It was obvious that Raj and his fellow-escapee had friends all over that area who took them food and warned them of any danger. Embarrassing as it was, the local police official asked Amy to try to persuade him to surrender. Did they think the missionary lady would ask him in a letter? Amy let her Indian servants know she wanted to meet Raj. She stained her arms and legs and put on her darkest sari. At midnight two men appeared at her bungalow and led her through the jungle to meet Raj. Amy pleaded with him to surrender.

'It was stupid to escape from prison,' he admitted, 'but it's too late now. I shall perish by the hand of those who are hunting for me,' Raj told her.

'I cannot bear the thought of you going to God with blood on your hands,' Amy told him. 'I could only bear your death if I heard that you had died without a weapon in your hand.'

Raj held her hands in his and said, 'Do not fear for us. Will God forsake us?'

They read from the psalms and prayed before Amy left them and returned home.

A few weeks later Raj and his men fell into a trap laid for them in their village. They fired to scare the police away. They then set fire to the house Raj was in. His band ran out of the house and tried to find another place to hide. This time, though, there was to be no escape for Raj. He leapt onto a bank of red earth and, after waving his gun three times around his head, threw it away. He stood in front of a tamarind tree and removed the long scarf covering his chest. He shouted to the police, 'You whose duty it is to shoot, shoot here!' They fired, but all their bullets went into the tree-trunk. The police all rushed upon him then, though they did not need to as he offered no resistance. Finally, one of them shot him through the head.

News of his death reached Amy when she was staying at the Forest House. Her first question was about his gun. When they told her he died without his gun in his hand, she felt satisfied. This troubled, daring man had died as a trusting Christian. However, rumours about his death and even a false version given out by the authorities, were believed, even by missionaries living further away. Amy was named and blamed for her part in it all, many doubting that Raj had lived a Christian, honest life after his final escape from prison.

Amy wanted the truth to be known, not for Raj, or her own reputation, but to give a true account of how God had answered prayer for Raj. She even went on stage for the first time in her life. In her local village she and an evangelistic band visiting there, advertised that they would give talks on the Great War and the life of Red Tiger. Amy faced a large, interested audience who listened intently as she described how Raj found faith in the Lord Jesus.

The House in Kalakadu

It was always a thrill to Amy to see Christians from Dohnavur starting work in Hindu villages. A house in Kalakadu, a village only six miles away, had been empty for three years. Indians living there believed it was haunted so no one would dare to live in it. When it was offered to Amy, she was delighted. May Powell and a nurse were planning a dispensary there. One afternoon, Amy went over in the car to check on building progress. Always one to check details, she walked over to look at the outside toilet. An Indian worker had mistakenly dug a large hole just inside the door, instead of at the back. In the gathering darkness Amy did not see this, slipped and fell awkwardly into the hole. When lifted out, she could not stand on her ankle.

She obviously needed specialist help. The only vehicle large enough to take someone lying down was a lorry, so she was laid on its floor. She was shaken and jolted for the forty-six miles to the main C.M.S. hospital. They found she had a dislocated ankle and a broken leg. For a woman of sixty-three this was a dreadful shock. Amy's first comment when the limb had been set was, 'I'm glad it was me and not May. She'll be free to start work in Kalakadu.' May visited Amy and told her the local gossip. 'I'm afraid the villagers are saying your accident proves the house is haunted. The Muslims didn't want us in their village so they are saying it was the curse of Allah on you.'

On her return home Amy found all walking difficult. Medical advice in 1931 was to have plenty of rest after an injury like hers. When she tried to walk she was in dreadful pain. Arthritis set in. Her children were so used to seeing her little figure dashing round the compound that they felt strange and lost in the months that followed. Amy, too, had not wanted to be disabled in this way. Nearly twenty years before, when healthy and busy, she had written a prayer in her journal: *Lord, teach me how to conquer pain. When my day's work is done on earth, take me straight Home. Do not let me be ill and a burden or anxiety to anyone. Let me not die of a lingering illness. Father, forgive me if this prayer is wrong.*

Everyone at Dohnavur prayed for their Amma's recovery. As the months turned into years and Amy could not leave her bungalow bedroom, she came to accept God's answer of 'no'. It was a lesson that she had learnt many years before and would have to learn again. After all, having brown eyes instead of blue had been of enormous help in mingling with Indian men and women. Amy's troubles turned out to be a valuable lesson for the children. They all saw how she dealt with problems and remembered her words, 'It is the trial of our faith,' she always said.

For the very first time, Amy's bedroom actually had a bed in it. Up till now she had always slept on a mat, like the Indians. Writing and prayer became her main occupations, now she could no longer work physically. Many books and letters left that bungalow and travelled all round the world. Some letters were only to be read after her death – personal messages to her girls.

As she could no longer stride out on her long forest walks, Amy brought some wildlife of her own into her room. Scamp was a snapping, snarling little terrier who certainly seemed to be 'wild life' to Amy's nurses. He had to be banished from the room for his excitable ways. A little puppy, Tess, came next and was friendly to everyone. Several cages of birds were hung up on the verandah as Amy enjoyed their colourful feathers and their singing. Another fall left her with a broken arm and a broken leg but, once these had healed, she went on writing. After this she could not walk, or kneel or sit. She had to stay in her bed all the time. She wrote thirteen books, many published in languages all over the world.

As there was a threat that the Japanese would invade from Singapore, a plan of evacuation was drawn up. They sent supplies up to the houses in the forest to be ready for an invasion. Many foods became expensive. Although Amy had always relied on God to supply their needs, her books told many more people about Dohnavur and brought in money. More volunteers also came to carry on helping the girls and boys saved from theatre and temple slavery.

During this time a friend came to visit Amy whom she hadn't seen for twenty-eight years. It was Blessing - the one Amy had always delighted to tease about her slow Indian style of walking. 'This is how you went, Amma,' Blessing joked. 'You did not walk or even run — you flew! You kept glancing at that little watch of yours, telling us, "Let's not waste any moments."' As Blessing acted out a pantomime of this at the side of her bed, Amy and her nurses burst out laughing.

World War Two ended without Dohnavur girls having to be evacuated. In 1947 India became independent of British rule. While momentous events such as these hit the headlines, Amy remained in her bungalow room. Missionaries and nurses came and went. Alison, a nurse from New Zealand, used massage and exercise to keep Amy's right shoulder and hand mobile. As her joints stiffened, Amy asked her for the truth. 'Will I be able to move these fingers again?' Alison had to tell her that she probably would not. 'I gave that hand to the Lord to use and now he has taken it again. If I cannot write, I will have to dictate for others to write down for me.'

When Alison was leaving for a break in New Zealand, Amy knew her own death was near. 'Alison, we won't meet again in this world. When you hear I have gone, jump for joy.'

Amy died in January 1951. She was buried in the garden at Dohnavur, like every member of the family. As no graves were ever marked, her friends could not go against her wishes to be treated the same. Instead, they placed a stone bird-table over her grave and inscribed on the base the word 'Ammai', the Tamil word for 'well-loved mother'.

But that was not the End

But that was not the end. This is a story without an ending. The Dohnavur Fellowship is still working in India. Amy, long ago, told the leaders she handed the work over to, 'When decisions have to be made, don't look back and wonder what I would have done. Look up, and see what our Lord and master would have you do.'

Today all the work is done by Indians themselves. Like Amy herself, they do not put out appeals for money. They ask their Heavenly Father in prayer. Also like Amy, none of them is paid a salary for all they do.

Girls now live in cottages, about fifteen in each, with a house-mother to take care of them. Now that the law really has put a stop to girls being sold to the temples, where do these girls come from? Like many Asian countries, in India parents much prefer a son to a daughter. One reason for this is that the dowry system, also banned by the government, still continues. The bride's parents have to give their future son-in-law a good sum in cash, gold jewellery, even television sets and gold watches in modern India. Abandoned little girls are brought to Dohnavur where they are loved and brought up in happy groups.

The little children still wave their coloured flags while singing hymns in the services. Now, though, they are all girls and the dresses they wear are much brighter and more colourful than the ones worn in the old days. The girls at Dohnavur today giggle when shown the dresses worn years ago. Children go to primary school till they are eleven when, by law, they have to go away to boarding-school. There are no boys and no babies.

At the dairy farm the cows are milked at 3 a.m. The milk is then taken to the kitchens where it has to be boiled. They still grow their own fruit and vegetables. There is still a hospital, with its own x-ray department and operating theatre. The two doctors see about two hundred people every day in out-patients as well as treating those on the wards. There is a laboratory and a dental surgery. People who cannot afford to pay for their medical treatment are never turned away. They may be Hindu, Muslim or Christian. In this open, loving way, modern Dohnavur is what Amy wanted it to be, a place of love.

She wrote a prayer, 'Lord, teach us to care. Give it to us to love, as you love all the nations. Help us to give as you gave, holding nothing back.'

She told her workers, 'Forget yourself in serving others. That is the way of joy.'

Amy Carmichael
Life Summary

Amy Carmichael was born in Northern Ireland. When she was seventeen years old the family left their seaside home to live in Belfast. Her father died shortly after the move. It was here that Amy first became involved with mission work. As a child she had often seen beggars and homeless children. Never the sort of person to stand by and watch she had to do something. She organised fund raisers to help underprivileged children who had to work in the mills.

As she grew older the desire for missionary work did not leave. Her friends didn't think that she was cut out to be a missionary because her health was fragile. However her friends had not taken God into account. Amy finally went to India and it was in the mountains near Bangalore that she discovered the work that would be the focus of the rest of her life. Amy set up a home for young girls who had been rescued from being slaves in Hindu temples. A house for boys was also built, and a community hospital.

Amy's rescue attempts earned her friends and enemies in India. But she continued to do this despite the danger it caused to her own life. She ran the homes and mission work for fifty-five years and it is still in operation today.

Thinking Further Topics

1. Into the Dark

Are you, or have you ever been scared of the dark? How do you think the little girl Jeya felt in this strange temple? Was she treated well by the temple workers? Amy Carmichael treated Jeya differently. What was the main difference between the temple workers and Amy? One group, were, of course, horrible and cruel to the little girl. They bought her from her mother and pretended that they would look after her – but they didn't. They beat her and left her in the temple on her own. They didn't love her or care for her. Amy, however, loved the little girl, and hundreds of other little girls just like her. She rescued Jeya from the temple workers and took her back to live with her. Amy cared for her. This shows us the difference between the false gods of the temple and the one true God that Amy worshipped. The false gods are evil and cruel and enslave people. The one true God is full of love, mercy and compassion. He rescues his people from fear and sin. He wants us to be part of his family. He sent his Son to the world to rescue sinners by dying in their place on the cross – taking their punishment for them. What a wonderful God he is.

(John 3:16)

2. Saved

Have you ever felt overwhelmed by problems? Have you ever felt that you are drowning in difficulties and worries?

Problems can come from lots of different places. Sometimes problems and bad things just happen. Life can be hard. Sin has made it that way. Read the story of Adam and Eve in the Bible to find out how it all happened. Amy had problems. God helped her when she was in danger in the boat. Can you think of some Bible characters who were in a boat when God helped them? (Noah; Peter and the disciples.) Some of Amy's problems however were of her own making. She foolishly ate the laburnum pods. But God looked after her then too. However, it is not always part of God's plan to sort out problems, difficulties and heartaches. Amy's father died. That was a very big problem and heartache. But God taught Amy that he would always be there for her. He is a father to the fatherless (Psalm 68:5) Look up the following scripture: Psalm 27:10. What does this verse tell us? (If either parent dies God will look after us.) Can you think of a difficulty or problem that God has used to teach you something? What did you learn?

3. The Shawlies

What do you think is more lasting? Gold, hay or stubble? Of course it is gold. If you set a match to all three the hay and the stubble will quickly disappear in a puff of smoke. But it wouldn't make much impact on the gold at all. Amy wanted to make sure that the things she did would last for eternity. But she could only do that if she depended on God. That is because what we do by ourselves is worth very little – it is God's power working in us and through us that is the work that will last. If you are a Christian the work that you do with God and for God is most important. Telling the good news of Jesus Christ to others, prayer, loving God, obeying his word – these are all tremendously important. They are all to do with our eternal life. They are precious. Following God's ways is like storing treasure in heaven – where rust doesn't corrupt or thieves break through and steal. If you do not love Jesus as your personal saviour the most important thing for you to do is to believe in the Lord Jesus Christ and you will be saved. (Acts 16:31) Your soul is the only bit of you that will last forever. It is eternal. Heaven and Hell are real places. God's love and God's judgement are real too. Trust in God completely. Today.

4. Sri-lanka, China, Hong-Kong, India

Do you think that you would like to dress in foreign clothes all the time? What about eating foreign food? What would you find hardest about moving to live in another country and culture? What would you miss? Amy's clothes took the old woman's mind off the gospel message. That is what made Amy think that she had to dress in native clothes. She didn't want people concentrating on what she was wearing rather than on what she was saying. Sometimes we can be distracted from the gospel too. The Good news of Jesus Christ is the most important thing that you will ever listen to. But sometimes our minds wander. Look up the following scripture: Luke chapter 8. What verses talk about people who are distracted or who have the message snatched away from them? (Look at verses 5&7 and then also verses 12&14.)

5. Tinnevelley

Do you see the results of racism in your own community? Do you hear about it on the news? Racism can take many disguises. Some people physically hurt others of a different nationality or skin colour. Some people won't be friends with people who are different to them. Some people make jokes about other people – and the jokes are often cruel. Racism is in most countries and cultures. What was the name that was given to the racist system in India when Amy was working there? (Hindu Caste system.) This is still prevalent in India today. One level of the Hindu caste system is called – Untouchables. If you are an untouchable, you are often despised. People avoid you. You are from the lowest caste if you are an untouchable. You get the worst jobs and you don't get access to education or health care in the same way that you might get it if you belonged to another higher caste. In Jesus' time there were people who were despised and rejected: Lepers and tax collectors and others. But Jesus befriended them. He cared for them. Do you only want to be friends with popular people or do you make a point of being friendly to new people, old people, people from different cultures and backgrounds?

6. The Woman who runs like a hare

Do you have a nickname? If you do, do you like it? If you don't have one or would like to change the one that you have, what nickname would you choose? What different characteristics do you have which make you unique and special? Everyone has something – you will have something too. Amy was called the woman who runs like a hare. She was pretty fast. Other Christian converts chose new names to reflect the kind of person that they wanted to be. One woman named Blessing said that it was better to have joy than to have learning. Is this always true? When is it true and when isn't it true? It is true when you are talking about having joy in Christ and salvation. That is certainly better than learning poetry or science or other things. But what if someone was joyful or happy about a new car, or clothes or other things but they had never learned about Jesus Christ? Joy can be real joy or false joy. The only real lasting joy is the joy that we get from following Jesus. Learning other subjects is valuable – but learning the truth of God is vital. Godly wisdom is different to being clever or passing exams. God can teach anyone to love him and follow him.

7. Pearl-eyes and the child stealer

Amy kept note of her prayers in an Ask and Receive book. Do you remember good things that happen to you? Do you keep a photograph or scrap book when you've been on holiday? Have good things that happened to you been in answer to prayer? If they have been, do you keep a special note of your answers to prayer? Amy and the mission workers prayed for a cheque of 100 rupees. It was more than they had ever received. Do you pray for things sometimes and think that it is too much to ask God for? Nothing is too much to ask God for. But remember he may answer – yes, no, or wait. In the meantime we have a lot to thank God for because every good and perfect gift comes from God. (James 1:17) He has given us so much. What do you want to give to him?

8. Amma

Have you ever wanted to change something about your appearance? Do you want to be taller; more beautiful; stronger? Perhaps you want to have long eyelashes, a less pointy chin, smaller ears? People often want to change their bodies but we don't often think about changing the real person inside. If you're a Christian you should be thinking about your life and how it needs to change to become more like the life of Christ. We should turn away from sin, obey God's word, become more like Christ in what we think, say and do. If you aren't a Christian you should change by asking Jesus to take control of your life. Our soul is more important than our body. Our character and our behaviour should be pleasing to God. Yes we should be concerned to an extent about the way we look. Are we tidy and clean? It is good to make our bodies physically fit and strong. And it isn't wrong to wear nice clothes or jewellery – but these things are not vital. They shouldn't be the most important things in life. God should be. Honouring and loving him should be vital to us.

9. A letter from a Queen

Do you have discussions about religion in your class? In some schools they talk about lots of religions. Though it is sometimes good for Christians to know about what other religions believe – we should never think that all the religions are the same. Jesus said, "I am the way, the truth and the life. No one can come to the Father except through me. (John 14:6) Jesus is not just one choice out of many, he is the only choice. Amy Carmichael saw the juggernaut procession in India where the people carried the false god, Vishnu, on a cart through the town. A naked man followed the cart rolling in the dirt. Police were there to stop people throwing themselves under the wheel of the cart. The people thought that this behaviour would ensure them a place in heaven. They thought it would please their god.

But Jesus is the only way to heaven. He is the truth. He is not one truth, or a truth. Truth is truth and if it's not truth it's a lie. Jesus never lied - his whole life was good. Can you think of some of the good things that Jesus did? He fed the hungry (John 6). He healed the sick (John 4). He gave sight to the blind (John 9) and even as he died he forgave those who hurt him and abused him (Luke 23). Jesus was sinless. In the scripture it says that there is 'none good but God.' (Matthew 19:17) 2 Corinthians 5:21 tells us that Jesus was made sin even though he was without sin. He did this to save us from sin. So as Jesus is pure and good we can conclude that he wasn't lying. In the last chapter of the New Testament we read the following words, 'These words are trustworthy and true.' (Revelation 22:6) Remember Jesus is the way, the truth and the life (John 14:6). So Jesus wasn't bad or a liar and he wasn't mad either – everything he did and does and is and was is full of wisdom. He always did exactly what was needed and said just the right words to the disciples, the pharisees and to people who needed his help. We must therefore believe that Jesus is who he claims to be – the Son of God. Jesus is telling the truth. He is the truth. Do you believe this?

10. Hundreds of Children

Amy made Ponnammal's funeral a celebration. Does that seem strange to you? Do you think it is right to do that in every situation? When might it be right to celebrate death and when is it wrong? When you read about Jesus weeping at the tomb of Lazarus does this make you think about death in a different way? (John 11) Jesus wept even though he knew that he would raise Lazarus back to life. This shows us that death is something that is upsetting. Human beings were never created to die. We were created to live – but it is our sin that has made the world and our lives this way – the way of death. In the Bible it does say to Christians however that we shouldn't be ignorant about people who die. We should not grieve like those people who have no hope because we do have hope. Those who love Christ go to be with him when they die. Whatever happens though – death is still painful and distressing. But for those who believe in Christ there is always hope – and our hope is sure and certain when we hope in Jesus. (1 Thessalonians 4:13; Hebrews 11:1)

11. Buying the Grey Jungle

Amy's plans blossomed. She bought the grey jungle and despite problems, she and the children eventually had a completed building of their own. They bought more land later on for a school but faced opposition. Have you ever faced opposition? Christians in many countries today have to struggle against the enemies of Christ. In schools you can be bullied or made fun of for being a Christian. But you will always face opposition when you follow Christ. The Bible tells us that the world hated Christ before it hated us and that men will hate us because of Christ. (Matthew 10:22) Amy's enemies didn't succeed in the end and the land purchase went ahead. You may struggle against bullies and other people who do not love the Lord – you may have to struggle for years. But God has promised that he will keep you strong to the end, 1 Corinthians 1:8.

12. Fear at the Theatre Schools

The aims of the fellowship that Amy founded were: To save children in moral danger. To train them to serve others. To care for the desolate and the suffering. To make known the love of our Heavenly Father especially to the people of India. What are your aims for your life? Do you have ambitions? Do you want to achieve certain things? There is nothing wrong in that. Just make sure that you are following Christ and trusting him to guide you. Ask his advice in prayer and ask him to show you what he wants you to do. Make the Lord Jesus Christ the unseen leader of your life as he was the unseen leader of the Dohnavur fellowship.

13. Celebrations

What things do you celebrate? What days of the year are special to you and why? Do you have special things that you do as a family on occasions like these? What emotions do you feel when you celebrate a special day or event? What days of the year do we have as specific celebrations connected to Jesus Christ? Many people celebrate his birth but do you celebrate his death? It may be strange to celebrate a death – but we have great reason to celebrate Christ's death. Why is this? It is because he died to save us from our sins and once victorious against sin, death and the devil – he rose from the dead and is now in heaven. Traditionally Christ's death is celebrated at Easter time. But does Christ's death and resurrection mean something special to you personally? Do you know that Jesus died for you? He is the perfect example of true love. People looked at Amy and saw her life as an example of how love suffers long and is kind (1 Corinthians 13). Jesus has suffered the most on the cross – and he was so kind to do that for us.

14. Just 260 Rupees

Isn't it amazing that God knows what we need – exactly! He knows how many hairs are on our heads too – even if we have none – or if we have rather more than the average! Do you have specific prayers or problems that you are struggling with at the moment? Pray to God about them and ask him for help. Be confident that he is the hearer and answerer of prayer.

Amy was given exactly 260 Rupees – it covered the exact amount of money they required for the work. It was very precise. Do you sometimes wonder if God even hears you? Do you sometimes wonder if he cares? Stop wondering. Be confident this God made the ear and he hears and he is love! Other loves are shadows in comparison to his.

15. The Robber Chieftain

The Robber Chieftain, Raj, and Robin Hood (a character from English folklore) and Jesus Christ were similar but different. Raj lived in India and through Amy's testimony we know he existed. We don't have the same proof for Robin Hood. Only one or two stories passed down the generations. With Jesus we have lots of truth – God's word to be precise. There are many eye witness accounts of his life and death and resurrection. Five hundred people are recorded as having seen him risen from the dead! Again – a precise number. Raj and Robin Hood are recorded as having been thieves. They stole from the rich and gave to the poor. Jesus didn't steal anything. He was sinless. But he was crucified between two thieves. Raj said that he was falsely accused and Amy believed that. But Raj had definitely done some wrong things, he had stolen goods and he had been violent. He may have been falsely accused about some things – but not all. Jesus was falsely accused when he had done no sin at all. Jesus took the punishment on the cross for the sins of others – including Raj's. But Jesus does give to the poor – in a better way than Raj did. He gives rich and poor alike forgiveness, salvation and eternal life – all we have to do is ask him. Perhaps you think that you aren't poor. But think for a moment – there are other ways that you can be poor as well as not having money. How can that be? You can be rich with money but poor in the eyes of God. You are poor spiritually if you do not trust in Jesus Christ.

16. The House in Kalakudu

God's answer to Amy's prayer for blue eyes had been no and he also answered no to her other prayer, "Do not let me be ill or a burden or anxiety to anyone." Do you pray? Do you pray to ask for things? Do you pray to say sorry? Do you pray to say thank you? This is all important in prayer to God. But prayer is really about building a relationship with God – a friendship. It is about finding out about God – how wonderful he is, how we should respect him and glorify him. God can speak to us too during our prayer times. He can also speak to us through his word the Bible. Amy died in 1951 and before that she told a friend that when she heard the news of her death she was to jump for joy. Joy is certainly the experience of every believer in Jesus Christ who finally comes home to heaven. When they meet with their Saviour face to face what a wonderful day that will be. He will then wipe away every tear from their eyes (Revelation 7:17)

17. But that was not the end

How is it that this story hasn't ended yet? What has changed at Dohnavur over the years? Why have these changes happened? Amy advised her staff to give without holding anything back. Amy was an example of this but Jesus is the perfect example. What did Jesus give for you? He gave his life. He suffered and died on the cross. He was separated from his Father. But today he is at his Father's right hand in heaven and one day his people will be there with him. That will be a day of real joy. Meanwhile we will serve others in the name of Christ for real joy on earth.

Prayer Suggestions

1. Find out about the country of India and pray for it. Thank God for the life of Amy Carmichael.

2. Pray for abandoned and orphaned children across the world. Ask God to send Christians to help and protect them.
Thank God for the people who love and take care of you.

3. Pray for girls born in countries where girls are not wanted as much as boys. Pray that attitudes in these countries will change. Thank God that he loves boys and girls just the same.

4. Pray for the persecuted church in India. Pray that Christians in India will show God's love to all people. Thank God that he loves rich and poor alike.

5. Pray to God for your family and friends. Ask God to help them to follow and obey him. Thank God for school and the chance to learn about the world and about him.

6. Pray to God for Bible translators who translate God's word so that people can read it for themselves in their own tongue. Thank God that you have access to Bibles.

7. Pray that God will give you a desire to serve him and not to hold back. Thank him that he gave his one and only son.

Amy Carmichael
Time Line

1852   Harriet Beacher Stowe: Uncle Tom's Cabin.

1854   Charles Dickens: Hard Times.

1857   The Indian Mutiny.

1860   Abraham Lincoln Elected President.

1861   Civil War breaks out in U.S.A.

1867   Amy Carmichael born.
        Karl Marx: Das Kapital.
        Alfred Nobel: Invents dynamite.

1876   Queen Victoria proclaimed Empress of India.
        Battle of Little Big Horn.
        Alexander Graham Bell: Invents telephone.

1879   Thomas Edison: Invents Electric bulb.
        Albert Einstein born.
        Amy starts boarding school.

1883   Brooklyn Bridge completed.

1885   Indian National Congress formed.

1889   Eiffel Tower designed.
        Amy's Hall 'The Welcome' is opened.

1890   First moving pictures shown.

1891   Russia begins to build Trans Siberian
        Railway.

1892   Amy Carmichael leaves for Japan.

1895   Amy sails for India.

1898   Marie Curie discovers radium and
        polonium.

1900   Australia becomes a commonwealth.

1901   Queen Victoria dies.

1902   The Teddy Bear introduced.

1903	Plague in India.
1904	Trans Siberian Railway completed.
1905	Albert Einstein: Theory of Relativity.
1906	Kelloggs start selling cornflakes.
1907	First electric washing machine invented.
1908	Ford introduces the Model T.
1909	Plastic invented.
1912	Sinking of the Titanic.
1913	Amy's mother dies.
1914	First World War begins.
1917	Russian Revolution.
	America enters World War I.
1919	World War I ends.
	Amy awarded *The Kaiser-I-Hind* medal for services to India.
1923	Talking movies invented.
1927	BBC founded.
	The Dohnavur Fellowship founded.
1928	Penicillin discovered.
1930	Pluto discovered.
1939	World War II begins.
1945	World War II ends.
1947	India becomes independent of British rule.
1949	First non-stop round the world flight.
1950	First credit card introduced.
1951	Amy Carmichael dies.
1953	D.N.A. discovered.
1961	Soviets launch first man in space.

John Welch
The Man Who Couldn't Be Stopped
Ethel Barrett

John Welch couldn't be stopped. When he was a boy he was independent, stubborn and had a mind of his own. It all ended in tears when he fell in with a gang of thieves. But then he met God. John left his sinful life and became a preacher. With God beside him no one could stand in his way – not even the King of England or the King of France!

This is the true story of one of Scotland's most adventurous preachers. As the son-in-law of another fiery Scot – John Knox – John Welch was bound to cause a stir – and he did! Find out about how he conquered ruffians, saved a town from the dreaded plague and even dodged a cannon ball!

Extra Features include: Maps, Quiz, Timeline, What was life like then? Fact Summaries.

ISBN 978-1-85792-928-7

Wilfred Grenfell
The Arctic Adventurer
Linda Finlayson

"Faster, faster!" Wilfred Grenfell called to the sledge team. The dogs needed no second reminder. They loved to go fast. Wilfred loved it too, and felt a thrill as the cold wind blew past his face. There was such freedom flying across deep snow and ice. But just then, instead of hard ice, they hit slush, which meant a patch of ice was melting and could break apart at any moment. "Come on," Wilfred yelled. "Faster!" But it did not matter. The worst thing happened. Right in front of the dogs the ice cracked open. One by one the dogs slid into the freezing water…..

Take part in this adventure that is the life of Dr. Wilfred Grenfell, missionary and medic to the frozen wastelands of Labrador and Newfoundland.

ISBN 978-1-85792-929-4

TRAILBLAZER SERIES

Gladys Aylward, No Mountain too High
ISBN 978-1-85792-594-4
Corrie ten Boom, The Watchmaker's Daughter
ISBN 978-1-85792-116-8
David Brainerd, A Love for the Lost
ISBN 978-1-84550-695-7
Paul Brand, The Shoes that Love Made
ISBN 978-1-84550-630-8
Billy Bray, Saved from the Deepest Pit
ISBN 978-1-84550-788-6
Bill Bright, Dare to be Different
ISBN 978-1-85792-945-4
John Bunyan, The Journey of a Pilgrim
ISBN 978-1-84550-458-8
Amy Carmichael, Rescuer by Night
ISBN 978-1-85792-946-1
John Calvin, After Darkness Light
ISBN 978-1-84550-084-9
Jonathan Edwards, America's Genius
ISBN 978-1-84550-329-1
Michael Faraday, Spiritual Dynamo
ISBN 978-1-84550-156-3
Billy Graham, Just Get Up Out Of Your Seat
ISBN 978-1-84550-095-5
Adoniram Judson, Danger on the Streets of Gold
ISBN 978-1-85792-660-6
Isobel Kuhn, Lights in Lisuland
ISBN 978-1-85792-610-1
C.S. Lewis, The Storyteller
ISBN 978-1-85792-487-9
Eric Liddell, Finish the Race
ISBN 978-1-84550-590-5

Martyn Lloyd-Jones, From Wales to Westminster
ISBN 978-1-85792-349-0

George Müller, The Children's Champion
ISBN 978-1-85792-549-4

Robert Murray McCheyne, Life is an Adventure
ISBN 978-1-85792-947-8

John Newton, A Slave Set Free
ISBN 978-1-85792-834-1

Mary of Orange, At the Mercy of Kings
ISBN 978-1-84550-818-0

John Paton, A South Sea Island Rescue
ISBN 978-1-85792-852-5

Helen Roseveare, On His Majesty's Service
ISBN 978-1-84550-259-1

Mary Slessor, Servant to the Slave
ISBN 978-1-85792-348-3

Charles Spurgeon, Prince of Preachers
ISBN 978-1-84550-155-6

Patricia St. John, The Story Behind the Stories
ISBN 978-1-84550-328-4

John Stott, The Humble Leader
ISBN 978-1-84550-787-9

Joni Eareckson Tada, Swimming against the Tide
ISBN 978-1-85792-833-4

Hudson Taylor, An Adventure Begins
ISBN 978-1-85792-423-7

John Welch, The Man who couldn't be Stopped
ISBN 978-1-85792-928-7

George Whitefield, The Voice that Woke the World
ISBN 978-1-84550-772-5

William Wilberforce, The Freedom Fighter
ISBN 978-1-85792-371-1

Richard Wurmbrand, A Voice in the Dark
ISBN 978-1-85792-298-1

Start collecting this series now!

Ten Boys who used their Talents:
ISBN 978-1-84550-146-4
Paul Brand, Ghillean Prance, C.S.Lewis,
C.T. Studd, Wilfred Grenfell, J.S. Bach,
James Clerk Maxwell, Samuel Morse,
George Washington Carver, John Bunyan.

Ten Girls who used their Talents:
ISBN 978-1-84550-147-1
Helen Roseveare, Maureen McKenna,
Anne Lawson, Harriet Beecher Stowe,
Sarah Edwards, Selina Countess of Huntingdon,
Mildred Cable, Katie Ann MacKinnon,
Patricia St. John, Mary Verghese.

Ten Boys who Changed the World:
ISBN 978-1-85792-579-1
David Livingstone, Billy Graham, Brother Andrew,
John Newton, William Carey, George Müller,
Nicky Cruz, Eric Liddell, Luis Palau,
Adoniram Judson.

Ten Girls who Changed the World:
ISBN 978-1-85792-649-1
Corrie Ten Boom, Mary Slessor,
Joni Eareckson Tada, Isobel Kuhn,
Amy Carmichael, Elizabeth Fry, Evelyn Brand,
Gladys Aylward, Catherine Booth, Jackie Pullinger.

Ten Boys who Made a Difference:
ISBN 978-1-85792-775-7
Augustine of Hippo, Jan Hus, Martin Luther,
Ulrich Zwingli, William Tyndale, Hugh Latimer,
John Calvin, John Knox, Lord Shaftesbury,
Thomas Chalmers.

Ten Girls who Made a Difference:
ISBN 978-1-85792-776-4
Monica of Thagaste, Catherine Luther,
Susanna Wesley, Ann Judson, Maria Taylor,
Susannah Spurgeon, Bethan Lloyd-Jones,
Edith Schaeffer, Sabina Wurmbrand,
Ruth Bell Graham.

Ten Boys who Made History:
ISBN 978-1-85792-836-5
Charles Spurgeon, Jonathan Edwards,
Samuel Rutherford, D L Moody,
Martin Lloyd Jones, A W Tozer, John Owen,
Robert Murray McCheyne, Billy Sunday,
George Whitfield.

Ten Girls who Made History:
ISBN 978-1-85792-837-2
Ida Scudder, Betty Green, Jeanette Li,
Mary Jane Kinnaird, Bessie Adams,
Emma Dryer, Lottie Moon, Florence Nightingale,
Henrietta Mears, Elisabeth Elliot.

Ten Boys who Didn't Give In:
ISBN 978-1-84550-035-1
Polycarp, Alban, Sir John Oldcastle
Thomas Cramer, George Wishart,
James Chalmers, Dietrich Bonhoeffer,
Nate Saint, Ivan Moiseyev,
Graham Staines.

Ten Girls who Didn't Give In:
ISBN 978-1-84550-036-8
Blandina, Perpetua, Lady Jane Grey,
Anne Askew, Lysken Dirks, Marion Harvey,
Margaret Wilson, Judith Weinberg,
Betty Stam, Esther John.

THE HISTORY LIVES SERIES
Let history come to life

Peril and Peace,
Chronicles of the Ancient Church
History Lives, Volume 1
ISBN: 978-184550-082-5

Monks and Mystics,
Chronicles of the Medieval Church
History Lives, Volume 2
ISBN: 978-1-84550-083-2

Courage and Conviction,
Chronicles of the
Reformation Church
History Lives, Volume 3
ISBN: 978-1-84550-222-5

Hearts and Hands,
Chronicles of the
Awakening Church
History Lives, Volume 4
ISBN: 978-1-84550-288-1

Rescue and Redeem,
Chronicles of the
Modern Church
History Lives, Volume 5
ISBN: 978-1-84550-433-5

CHRISTIAN FOCUS PUBLICATIONS

Christian Focus | Christian Heritage | CF4K | Mentor

Christian Focus Publications publishes books for adults and children under its four main imprints: Christian Focus, CF4K, Mentor and Christian Heritage. Our books reflect that God's word is reliable and Jesus is the way to know him, and live for ever with him.

Our children's publication list includes a Sunday school curriculum that covers pre-school to early teens; puzzle and activity books. We also publish personal and family devotional titles, biographies and inspirational stories that children will love.

If you are looking for quality Bible teaching for children then we have an excellent range of Bible story and age specific theological books.

From pre-school to teenage fiction, we have it covered!

**Find us at our web page:
www.christianfocus.com**